AND ITS CLOSURE

The 09.30 Brighton to Horsham hauled by a Standard Class 8000 tank on Saturday, 11th April 1964. The train will have just passed the level crossing and Old Toll Bridge. Prominent on the skyline opposite is the Chapel of Lancing College. *Photo: M. Hudson.*

JAMES BUCKMAN

S. B. Publications

For Alastair, Matthew, Alice, George and Harry

First published in 2002 by James Buckman
in association with S.B. Publications
19 Grove Road, Seaford, East Sussex BN25 1TP
Tel: 01323 893498

ISBN 1 85770 254 9

Designed and Typeset by EH Graphics, East Sussex (01273) 515527
Printed by Pageturn Ltd, East Sussex (01273) 821500

Front Cover: The illustration on the front cover shows a former LBSCR 'K' Class locomotive No. 32359 heading a Sussex Special Rail Tour on the Steyning line, approaching Bramber from the south at approximately 17.15 on 7th October 1962. The train had left Preston Park Station at Brighton at 16.52, was due to arrive at Horsham at 17.41 and would then have proceeded via Dorking to London Bridge. Photo: *Courtesy and permission of Philip Barnes and 'Colour Rail'.*

Back Cover: This photograph shows the LBSCR signal box at Steyning, the 'candy twist' gas lamp column at the end of the Up platform, a typical Southern Railway signal column made of old rails welded together, the water column, a S.R. loading gauge over the adjoining goods yard siding and proceeding in the middle distance is a train which has just departed from the Up platform bound for Horsham. The closed corridor connection on the rear coach is indicative of the high quality of travel on the Steyning line. Photo: *M. S. Loader.*

CONTENTS

ACKNOWLEDGMENTS

I am greatly indebted to many people for their advice, help and encouragement. Messrs M. Chapman, R. Clay, D. Emsley and D. Freakes gave valuable help with the processing of data yielded by a card survey of users of the Steyning line in the autumn of 1965. At that time also, Steyning Parish Council kindly made information available and Mr. N.D. Wilson, Chief Traffic Officer of Southdown Motor Services subsequently gave time in an interview and information by letter on more than one occasion.

I am grateful to Professor Peter Haggett at Bristol for inspiration and some very useful ideas when the thesis mentioned in the Prologue was being prepared, enabling much that is in this book to be written. Thanks are also due to the General Manager of the former British Rail's Southern Region for permission to examine records at Waterloo and East Croydon. In particular, Mr F.W. Glassborow and Mr W.G.Owen helped by facilitating my work at that time in their departments.

My thanks also to Philip Barnes, Norman Checkley, George Cockman, Ian Denning, Philip Gardner, Simon Harrison, Bernard Holden, Mrs Joyce Sleight, Ronnie Stillwell, Chris' Tod of Steyning Museum and to Kenneth Stotesbury for some very practical help. To Mrs Oakey my thanks for permission to include in Chapter 1 her late husband's delightful sketch of the Whitehorse Hotel and to Mr John Sleight who generously offered the impressive photograph he took in his youth from the signal box at Beeding Cement Works, when the Steyning line was still operational. And not least my wife for her forbearance in many ways including help with our newly acquired computer.

Finally, my thanks to Mr Stephen Benz of S. B. Publications for his encouragement, advice and patience in waiting for the book's final draft.

If I have overlooked any person who has been a help, particularly in the matter of photographs, I ask forgiveness.

PROLOGUE

Breathes there the man, with soul so dead,
Who never to himself has said,
This is my own, my native land!
Whose heart has ne'er within him burned,
As home his footsteps he has turned
From wandering on a foreign strand?

Sir Walter Scott

December 1962 in the Punjab of Pakistan

An Englishman stood on the platform of Lahore railway station and glanced at some packing cases placed where they could most easily be loaded by red-clad porters into the luggage van of the Tez Gam ("The Flyer"). Each was marked in bold, black letters:

STEYNING, SUSSEX, ENGLAND

It was a moving moment, for the diesel-hauled train from Rawalpindi was rolling in. The man turned to his bearer and friends to say goodbye. Ten years earlier he had arrived in that land to help start and run a new school. Now, with extended contracts ended, he was going home.

January 1963

After a three week voyage from Karachi, calling at Aden, Port Said and Gibraltar, with Christmas celebrations on board, Anchor Line's RMS 'Cilicia' docked in Liverpool in one of the coldest winters the British Isles had known since that of 1947. It was late evening on Tuesday 1st January. Passengers spent a warm night on board and cleared Customs the following morning. With electrification of the west coast main line in progress, the journey south was to be from Birkenhead by express train to Paddington. In spite of frozen points, there were few delays caused by the freezing weather, and on the evening of the 2nd, the man arrived in Brighton Station to find he was in time to catch the last train that would be running that day to Steyning.

Through the snow drifts of the Adur Valley the three-coach train panted to its destination. Of the passengers alighting, one was a traveller at the end of a journey of 8,000 miles. The friendly Station Master telephoned the local garage, Woods of Steyning, for a taxi. Within a few minutes it arrived and five minutes after that the man was home.

AUTHOR'S NOTE

The reader may have guessed that the author of this book was the man referred to in the Prologue.

After returning to the United Kingdom, my first teaching appointment was a temporary one at Hampton where in addition to teaching geography, such rowing skills as I may have still had from my University days came into play, coaching the Colts VIII. During the summer term which saw Hampton's 1st VIII reaching the semi-finals of the Princess Elizabeth Cup at Henley, I was offered a permanent post at Brighton, Hove and Sussex Grammar School within twelve miles of Steyning. This would enable me to live at home and commute by train from Bramber to Brighton. The half mile (10 minute walk) at each end of the journey would make possible two miles' brisk walking each day, Monday to Saturday. It seemed ideal.

Then the Beeching Report was published. The Steyning line was cited as one which only carried 5,000 passengers a week (in fact, over 12,000 people used it) and therefore was one of those the Railways Board proposed to axe. Could a case of hardship be proved?

A comparison of train and bus journey times between Bramber and Brighton indicated that if recourse had to be made to travelling by bus, in a school year of 40 weeks which included Saturdays, the equivalent of an additional 33 eight hour working days would have to be added to the time already spent in travel by train. In that case, a car would have to be used; but it seemed worth making a bid for truth and sanity to prevail.

So a letter was written to the Secretary of the Transport Users' Consultative Committee setting out the facts. A copy of the letter went to the Chairman of Steyning Parish Council, Mr. D. Toomey, who had asked objectors also to write to him.

One Autumn evening, I received a call from Toomey, accompanied by Counsel who was to represent local authorities at the impending public inquiry. They asked if I would vet all copies of the objections which had been received, to see how each could be expressed in precise statistical terms, as mine had been. This proved virtually an impossible task; but two years' later, when Tom Fraser, as Minister of Transport consented to the closure, a card survey was devised which produced in moderate measure the precise information needed. As a result, I found myself closely involved in the local endeavour to save the Steyning line. We all hoped that Barbara Castle, who had taken over as Minister of Transport, would legislate to reverse Fraser's decision. But in the light of the information conveyed to her by our Member of Parliament, Henry Kerby, she only laid on extra buses which hardly anyone used. Nevertheless, a sequel was a suggestion from Professor Peter Haggett, Head of the School of Geographical Sciences at Bristol University, to incorporate the data yielded for a Master's thesis. In due time this was accomplished, its title being 'The Locational Effects of a Railway Closure'.

Friends have since urged me to use the material in a book and so, although thirty years have gone by, these pages are an attempt belatedly to fulfil their hopes and expectations.

INTRODUCTION

This book is about one of many parts of Britain's rail network closed in the 1960s. It was a vital resource for the communities it served and is of interest because the south east of Great Britain, the region in which the line used to function, is one of the major growth regions of the country, having rising population pressure. In the context of the national economy the region is seen to have a vital role in terms of industrial location because:

"A third of the employed population of Great Britain works in the South East Region. Industry in the South East contributes a major proportion of the country's exports and the region is often claimed to be the seed-bed for the development of new firms and industries How the economy of the South East is managed determines to a large extent how the national economy as a whole is managed".

As far as transport is concerned, the same body pointed out that

"..the relevance to intra-regional planning of the very extensive amount of shorter distance movement has not been appreciated in the past".[1]

One illustration of this is the relatively large number of railway closures in areas of large and increasing transport demand. Perhaps the supreme example of these follies perpetrated in the 1960s, ostensibly to save taxpayers' money, was well described in a letter to *'The Daily Telegraph'* of 28 September 1965, a few months before the Steyning line, the subject of this book, was closed.

In their letter, Lord Lanesborough and Peter R.J.Walker commented:

"...Among the main lines in the process of closure, surely the prize for idiotic policy must go to the destruction of the until recently most profitable railway per ton of freight and per passenger carried in the whole British Railways system, as shown by their own operating statistics. These figures were presented to monthly management meetings until the 1950s, when they were suppressed as "unnecessary," but one suspects really "inconvenient" for those proposing Beeching type policies of unnecessarily severe contraction of services..... This railway is of course the Great Central forming a direct Continental loading gauge route from Sheffield and the North to the Thames valley and London for Dover and France..."

In November 2001, the Commission for Integrated Transport, in its Report to H. M. Government, stated that Britain has the worst traffic congestion in Europe while the Confederation of British Industry reckoned that *"delays and logistical problems... are costing UK business £20 billion per year"*.[2]

An earlier review of transport policy in the United Kingdom forecast gridlock on the nation's roads by 2020 AD, so the policy of closing established rail links in regions of growth appears to be anomalous. If gridlock happens, a contributory factor will have been the axing of many parts of Britain's nationalised rail network, contributing little, if any, to the profitability of the railway industry. The unforeseen legacy of this in the South East and in many other parts of the United Kingdom has been to create traffic and public transport problems that are not easily solved.

On the positive side, one part of the nation's rail network from which passenger services had been withdrawn in 1964 has been reopened - the Robin Hood line, a 32 mile link between Nottingham and Worksop. With 3,000 passengers a day using it, the line now carries one of the most heavily loaded rail services in the East Midlands. And, according to a report in the *Sunday Telegraph of 6th May, 2001,* 34 years after it was abandoned, the cross-country rail link between Cambridge and Oxford is also to be restored in a £200 million scheme of

Britain's now privatised rail industry.

The railway, which is the subject of this book, linked two main lines and two conurbations, one which extends from Brighton to Worthing on the South Coast, the other centred on Crawley and extending from Horsham to Gatwick Airport. The route between the junctions in the parish of Itchingfield and Shoreham-by-Sea was 27.6 kilometres (17.3 miles) in length, double-tracked throughout and at one time was to have been electrified.

Traversing the gently undulating country of the southern Weald, the line reached the coast by utilising the gap through the South Downs formed by the River Adur. There were no tunnels and, save for cuttings in greensand at Henfield and Steyning, for the greater part of its route south of Partridge Green, the line lay on flat ground formed by the silting up of the Adur estuary. On this section, the hazard of possible flooding was effectively overcome by constructing the formation on a low embankment, with culverts bridging drainage channels.

While the book's narrative opens with the first chapter explaining to the reader why and how the line came to be built, its central core consists of an outline of passenger traffic revealed by census counts, the trend of ticket sales between 1948 and 1965 and some of the returns from a survey of users carried out shortly before passenger services were withdrawn. This is followed by an examination of the rationale of closure and then by the probable reasons for the closure having accelerated the decrease in the numbers of people using public transport - to an extent greater than may reasonably be explained solely by car ownership.

With a lack of interchange facility between buses and trains, it was inevitable that traffic volume on the Steyning line in the pre-closure period would be unlikely to reach its potential. This led to British Rail's policy of closure being implemented without further consideration. The narrative concludes by drawing the reader's attention to the possibility of how an integrated public transport network might have been established. One major consequence of the line's closure is that, for the foreseeable future, this is unlikely to be accomplished in that part of West Sussex the Steyning line once served.

[1] South East Joint Planning Team

[2] Report in the Sunday Telegraph, 23rd November, 2001

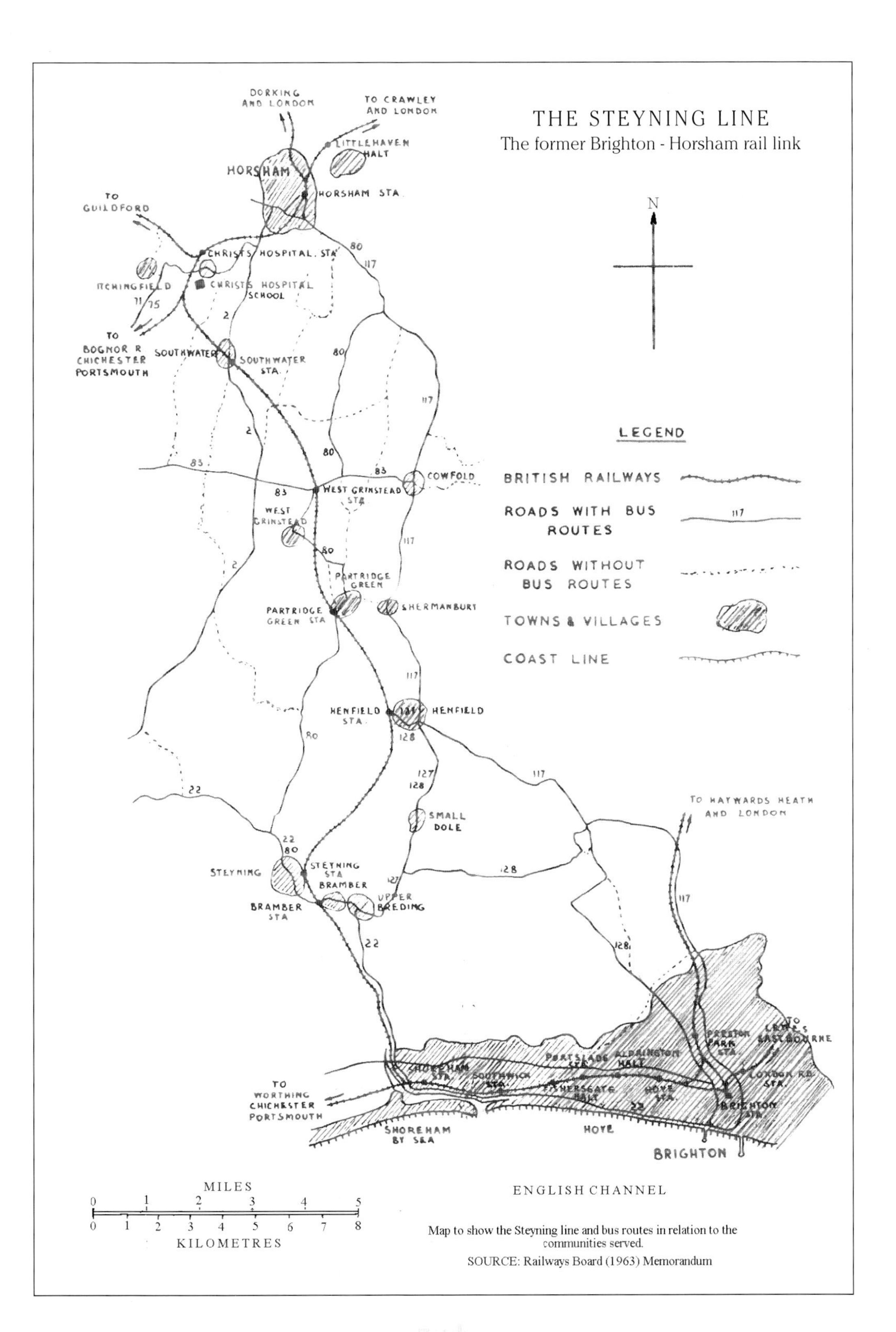

Map to show the Steyning line and bus routes in relation to the communities served.

SOURCE: Railways Board (1963) Memorandum

1 THE ESTABLISHMENT OF THE STEYNING LINE

The Nineteenth Century Railway Boom

Britain's railway system, which developed in the nineteenth century, was virtually complete by 1852 and until well into the twentieth century was the mode of transport par excellence. The internal combustion engine was not invented until towards the end of the century and a hundred years were to elapse before motorised vehicles on roads were to become a serious rival to the train. In his discussion of the early days of railways and economic growth in the United Kingdom, Reed explains that railways developed in Britain to carry existing traffic. This was usually set forth in detail in the prospectuses of new companies, though freight traffic did not always fulfil expectations. However, it is significant, as Reed points out: "... it was the stage-coaches rather than the canals, the passenger carriers rather than the freight carriers, which were supplanted the earlier and more completely." The reasons for this may be accounted for by the fact that, "... the coming of the railway to Britain did not lead to 'a wavelike profusion (of routes) of many sorts' simply because these were already flowing in established channels. The railways took over those channels, partially at first, almost entirely in the long run. They provided a better and cheaper service in most cases but they did not to any significant extent simply make possible what had previously been impossible".

Whereas railways were able to attract traffic by their superior speed, comfort and convenience, it was their profitability which was a main cause of their rapid expansion over the face of Britain. For, as has been asked, "... what could be more tempting than these new railways, with the Liverpool and Manchester paying 10% in 1836 and the Stockton and Darlington raising its dividend from 11 to 14 per cent in 1837? "

There was a ferment throughout the land, as increasing numbers of people sought a likely profitable investment of their savings. This was in addition to an almost universal demand that as many communities as possible might enjoy the new technology of transport. The major companies who had responsibility to their shareholders for the wise use of capital subscribed, were augmented by entrepreneurs whose business was the building and selling of railways, of whom Thomas Brassey is perhaps the most famous. Robert Stephenson, Locke and Brunel were the three outstanding engineers who were consultants to a number of enterprises and often Brassey entered into contracts with them. It was while Brunel's broad gauge main line linking Bristol with London was still under construction (opened in 1835), that the curtain rises on plans to connect England's southern coast with the Metropolis.

The 14.30 from Brighton to Horsham approaching Copsale to the north of West Grinstead on 30th April 1964. The train consisting of former Southern Railway main line corridor stock is being hauled by an Ivatt 2-6-2 tank No. 41326. *John Scrace*

The London to Brighton Main Line

In the year 1834 a group of citizens and merchants, wishing to promote a railway between Brighton and London, invited proposals and estimates from engineers to be submitted to them. The man they appointed to advise them was Robert Stephenson. After examining various proposals, he was most in favour of a route drawn out by an engineer named Cundy. However, because he saw some imperfections in Cundy's scheme, Stephenson surveyed a route of his own using river gaps through the North and South Downs. This he submitted to the Brighton Committee under his own name.

Five schemes, one of them Stephenson's, then went in the year 1836 for examination before a committee of the House of Commons. Each of the schemes was rejected, only to be revived in the following year. At this stage the rival concerns engaged in a fierce legal battle. As it became protracted, the Committee Chairman suggested that matters might best be brought to a conclusion if the Government were to appoint an independent arbitrator. This was agreed to and pending reference to Captain (later Colonel) Alderton of the Royal Engineers, who was to be entrusted with the task, the five companies agreed to amalgamate their interests into one Company and adopt whichever line Captain Alderton should recommend.

After surveying the routes proposed, Alderton prepared and submitted his report to the House of Commons Committee. This report recommended that the one submitted by Sir John Rennie, the "direct" route and the present-day main line, should be the one to gain Parliamentary sanction. Although one of the merits of Stephenson's route, which Alderton acknowledged, was its avoidance of tunnelling by using river gaps and its relative low cost per mile, journey times, fares and freight charges would have been higher because it would have required nearly seventy miles of railroad in addition to fourteen miles already constructed. By adopting the "direct" route, only forty-two miles of additional construction would be needed.

The second reason concerned possible extensions to the route in the future by building branches. On this point, Alderton wrote that Stephenson "did altogether exclude Lewes and the port of Newhaven."

Had Stephenson's route been adopted, the London to Brighton main line would have missed that opportunity while its route, having passed through Leatherhead, Dorking and Horsham, would have taken it down the Adur valley, past Henfield and Steyning to Shoreham-by-Sea.

The London and Brighton Railway (LBR) was the Company that built the "direct" line to Brighton and, using the port of Shoreham, in 1840 opened the short stretch of line along the coast through Hove to bring in materials for its southern end. With the completion of work on Clayton Tunnel the main line between London and Brighton came into service on 21st September 1841.

Branch from proposed Portsmouth line

Three years later, in 1844, the London and South Western Railway (LSWR) promoted a scheme for a line to Portsmouth. Robert Stephenson was one of their consultant engineers and again the alignment for the proposed railway took it via the Mole Gap through the North Downs to serve Dorking, Horsham, Arundel and Chichester. Also, from a point near Horsham, a branch was proposed to run due south to Shoreham which, because of its port, was a major attraction. The branch envisaged would have gone through the South Downs by using the Adur Gap with Henfield and Steyning the beneficiaries. The Minutes of the Court of Directors of the LSWR indicate that the branch was "determined upon but surveys may be necessary".

Branch from coast line at Shoreham

On learning of the LSWR's proposed branch into their territory at Shoreham, the Directors of the London and Brighton Railway viewed with concern the threat to their monopoly of access to the South Coast. They decided to counter it with all speed and on 5th November 1845, resolved "that a line from Shoreham to Steyning be surveyed and the requisite Parliamentary notices given". A Bill that allowed the London & Brighton Railway to proceed with their Steyning and other branches received the Royal Assent on 18th June 1846. On 15th July, the Company's resident engineer, R. Jacombe-Hood, was "...instructed to examine the Parliamentary lines for the several Branches and report on the best mode of carrying them into execution;...and that the Keymer, Newhaven and Steyning branches be first proceeded with...".

Twelve days later, the London and Croydon Railway was amalgamated with the London and Brighton Railway and so there was a new Board of Directors of what then became the London, Brighton and South Coast Railway (LBSCR). The instructions previously given to Hood were confirmed and the Minutes for 23rd September 1846 state: "Read Mr Hood's Report... on the Steyning Branch where considerable difficulty presented itself from the Agreement with the Shoreham and Steyning Turnpike Road Trustees binding this Company to take the road under the Railway, a thing practically impossible, as the road must be lowered below the bed of the river running within twenty yards of it." The problem was eventually resolved when, on 2nd December 1846, the imperative which gave to the Steyning Branch equal ranking with the Keymer and Newhaven Branch schemes abruptly ceased.

The LSWR Court had on 20th November instructed their Engineer and Solicitor to abandon all proceedings with reference to the Godalming, Chichester and Portsmouth line -

A view of Shoreham's Old Toll Bridge from the west bank of the River Adur, pre-1965, when it carried the traffic of the A27, crossing the Steyning line on the further side. The Church of St. Nicholas, Old Shoreham, the birthplace of Lancing College can be clearly seen. Photo: *E. Wilmshurst.*

and the branch to Shoreham. This was because there had been a deterioration in the nation's economy, resulting in a deep recession. The LBSCR Directors were then in much less haste to promote the Steyning branch and on 15th November 1847 the project was shelved. The reasons for doing so were clearly financial for Hood's Diary records:

2nd October 1847	Company in financial difficulties; ordered to stop all new works in progress and to reduce wages.
28th November 1847	Received Notice to leave and ordered to give Notice to Staff, with a view to general reduction.
3rd January 1848	Sent in resignation, which was accepted.
18th March 1848	Reappointed Engineer.

The financial stringency of those times is also indicated in the Minutes of a Parliamentary Inquiry of 1858 and this includes some evidence of Samuel Laing, who had been Chairman of the London and Brighton Railway before that Company was amalgamated with the London and Croydon Railway in 1846. Asked by Burke to explain the circumstances in which powers to construct branches had been abandoned, Laing said, "They were abandoned during the crisis of 1847 and 1848 when Railway property was almost irretrievably ruined and it was absolutely impossible to raise money."

It is clear that the LBSCR's financial difficulties were no less acute in 1847 than the LSWR's had been a year earlier, or they may have delayed action because of the smaller and less expensive project with which they were concerned. Be that as it may, Dyos and Aldcroft add their description of the malaise in the nation's economy:

"In two scarcely unexpected movements during the spring and summer of 1847 the financial crisis came dramatically to its head, bank rate moved almost to panic level, and the whole frenzied mood of an over-stretched market was finally relaxed. So far as the railways were concerned this, too, was the end for the time being of their tearaway promotion of the

previous four years".

Nine years were now to elapse before the LBSCR Minutes were to have recorded in them any indication that a line to serve Steyning was contemplated.

The Steyning Railway Company

In the year 1856, some residents of Steyning and its neighbourhood decided to form a Company which would construct a line of railway to link Steyning with the LBSCR's coast line at Shoreham. The Meeting, which adopted the project, was held in Steyning's White Horse Hotel on 23rd June. They approached the Board of the LBSCR who agreed conditionally to lease the line from the Steyning Company after they had had it built by a contractor. The terms agreed included a rent of 4% of the Steyning Company's capital outlay. Jacombe-Hood was instructed to survey the route and report on traffic potential. His Report was submitted to the Board on 21st August 1856. The first part of his Report was an estimate of costs and the second an outline of goods and cattle traffic which the reader will find in the context of Chapter 3.

Hood's estimate made no provision for a viaduct over the River Adur and, because the traffic survey refers specifically to a station near Applesham Farm close to the new Lancing College, it is clear that the proposed alignment lay entirely on the west bank of the river. Hood's estimate of the cost of constructing the line was for a sum of £39,000. Before work could begin it was necessary that the Steyning Company should have raised 75% of the cost. This was nearly achieved but four months later they were still £7,890 short of the total and on 4th December John Ingram, the Company's Secretary, reported this position to the LBSCR and asked whether the larger Company would "undertake to provide at the proper time the requisite balance of Capital". To arrive at a decision the LBSCR Chairman, Leo Schuster accompanied by Admiral Laws, a fellow Director, went over the route personally on 12 December 1856. Schuster's report on the 18th was:

"that the project was not of sufficient importance as should induce this Company to deviate from the terms which they have already undertaken to enter into".

With this refusal, the Steyning Company decided to abandon their intended application to Parliament. The Brighton Minutes of the 8th January conclude:

"... that this Board will at the proper time be prepared to take the question of a Steyning line again into their consideration, with a view to meeting the reasonable requirements of that District".

Eight months later they had to consider the matter afresh. This was sooner than they appear to have expected and it was to be at greater cost.

The Landowners' Project of 1857

Stephenson's route, which the LSWR had abandoned eleven years earlier, formed the basis of proposals published in Steyning on 5th September 1857. The moving spirit, again, was John Ingram. The Memorandum which bore his name stated that the project was "promoted and supported as an independent scheme by the Landowners and Residents in the District" and was "wholly unconnected with the Brighton Company". The new enterprise called itself the SHOREHAM HORSHAM AND DORKING RAILWAY COMPANY and its Bill received a Second Reading in Parliament on 10th February 1858. As Engineer, the promoter had the services of Joseph Locke, ranked by Walker with the Stephensons and Brunel as one of the great railway engineers of his time. With Thomas Brassey as Contractor, described by Walker as "one of the giants of the nineteenth century..." it was no feeble enterprise which the Committee of the House of Commons now had to consider.

The London, Brighton and South Coast Railway's Scheme

The first occasion on which the directors of the LBSCR were officially informed of the projected Landowners' (or Mr. Locke's) line was at a meeting of the Board on lst October 1857. This was followed by a resolution to apply to Parliament for powers to construct a line from Shoreham to Steyning and Henfield.

Some six weeks later, the Board received Hood's estimates for their proposed line if it was extended to join the Mid-Sussex line at Billingshurst. The public were greatly interested in the project and on 24th December of the same year the Company's Secretary was instructed to write to the Hon. Mr. Brand in reply to an inquiry he had made about the proposed route. This reply was to the effect that:

"... it certainly is the intention of this Board to construct the entire line from Shoreham to Billingshurst, provided they can obtain the sanction of Parliament to the Bill."

The promotion of two rival schemes involved an expensive legal battle and a Parliamentary Inquiry in order to determine, on their merits, which of the two schemes should pass into law. The Minutes of the Inquiry mention that Walter Barseller, a magistrate and director of the Mid-Sussex Railway, was called to give evidence. He told the Committee that the reason for the proposed alignment to Billingshurst was "the probability of the extension of the proposed line towards Guildford". A fellow magistrate, Mr William Cory confirmed this, and that from Billingshurst the preferred route would be by way of Loxwood. The outcome of the Inquiry is referred to in the Minutes of the Brighton Company for 6th May 1858. These include the following entry:

"Mr G Gaithfull, Jnr., (the Company's Solicitor) reported that the Shoreham, Horsham and Dorking Bill was yesterday thrown out by the Committee of the House of Commons and that the preamble of this Company's Bill had been declared to have been proved."

After Parliament's sanction had been obtained a development, which had not been anticipated, prompted reconsideration of the direction the new line was to take. It transpired that another company, the Direct Horsham and Guildford Railway, was in its early planning stage and would most likely be built. Consequently, instead of going towards Billingshurst, Jacombe-Hood was now instructed to survey a route which deviated north of Partridge Green so that it would join the Mid-Sussex line close to the southern end of the projected link between Guildford and Horsham in the parish of Itchingfield (See Fig 1.1). Hood's survey of the whole route up to its junction with the Mid-Sussex line at Itchingfield having been completed, construction of the line began in the summer of 1859 by the contractor, Mr. Firbank, and the first section, that between Shoreham and Partridge Green, opened to traffic on 1st July 1861.

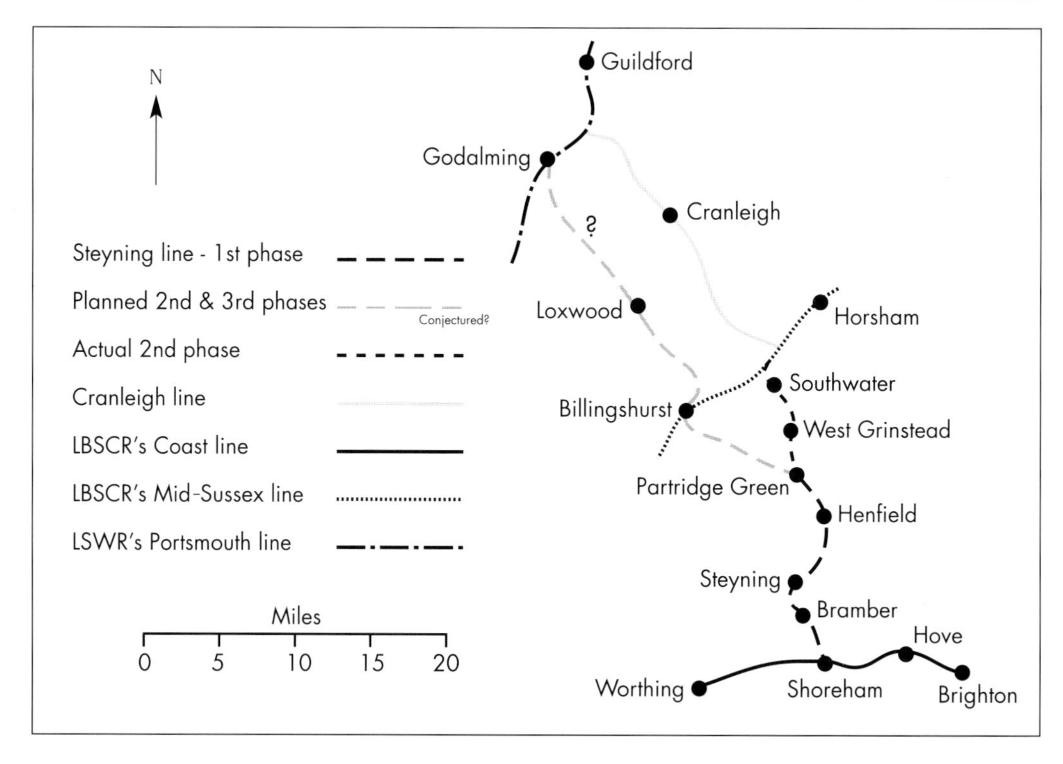

Fig. 1.1 Developments in the projected rail link between Brighton and Guildford.

Fig 1.2 is a facsimile of a public notice announcing the opening of the line which for many years was on display in the former Bramber Museum. The reader's interest may focus on the details it gives of fares and times of trains which were to run three times daily.

Included in the West Sussex Gazette's report of the opening was the following item:

THE DAY THE RAILWAY CAME

"...a few days before the opening the Government Inspector of Railways, Colonel Tyler, made a minute inspection of the new line, testing in particular the strengths of several bridges across the Adur. To examine the train worthiness of the long bridge across the river at Beeding cement works, four railway engines with their tenders attached, were placed on it...After their successful test, the Colonel and his party adjourned to celebrate at The White Horse in Steyning."

Conclusion

Having now reviewed the historical developments, which led to the building of the Steyning line, the reader will be in a position to assess the reasons for them.

The first was when there was a possibility that the route of the main line from London to Brighton, advocated by Robert Stephenson, would have passed through the Adur Gap of the South Downs and thus served the communities of Henfield and Steyning.

The second was when the London and South Western Railway wished to tap additional sources of traffic by running a branch line to Shoreham from near Horsham on its projected Chichester and Portsmouth line. The third was a response to the second. In this instance, the London and Brighton Railway (the precursor of the LBSCR), finding itself threatened by the proposed incursion into its territory, promoted a Bill for a branch line from Shoreham to Steyning, in the path of the line it was designed to counter.

London, Brighton, and South Coast Railway.

THE

SHOREHAM,

STEYNING & HENFIELD

LINE

WILL BE OPENED FOR PUBLIC TRAFFIC

(Passengers and Goods) on

MONDAY, July 1st

1861

TRAINS WILL RUN BETWEEN

PARTRIDGE GREEN AND BRIGHTON

AS UNDER:

All Trains 1st, 2nd, and 3rd Class.

From Brighton.	Week Days.			Sundays.			Fares from Brighton. Single Tickets.			
	a.m.	p.m.	p.m.	a.m.	p.m.	p.m.	1st. s. d.	2nd. s. d.	3rd. s. d.	Parly s. d.
Brighton (departure)	7 15	1 50	6 30	8 0	2 30	6 30				
Portslade	7 22	1 57	6 37	8 7	2 37	6 37	0 8	0 6	0 4	0 3
Southwick	7 25	2 0	6 40	8 10	2 40	6 40	0 9	0 7	0 5	0 4
Kingston	7 30	2 5	6 45	8 15	2 45	6 45	0 10	0 8	0 5	0 5
Shoreham	7 35	2 10	6 50	8 20	2 50	6 50	1 0	0 9	0 6	0 5
Bramber	7 45	2 20	7 0	8 30	3 0	7 0	2 1	1 7	1 0	0 10
Steyning	7 48	2 23	7 3	8 33	3 3	7 3	2 2	1 8	1 1	0 10
Henfield	7 58	2 33	7 13	8 43	3 13	7 13	3 0	2 3	1 6	1 2
Partridge Green (arrival)	8 5	2 40	7 20	8 50	3 20	7 20	3 4	2 6	1 8	1 4

From Partridge Green.							Fares from Brighton. Return Tickets			
	a.m.	p.m.	p.m.	a.m.	p.m.	p.m.	1st	2nd.	3rd.	Parly
Partridge Green (departure)	8 15	3 0	8 0	9 0	3 30	8 0	6s. 0d	3s. 9d.	2s. 6d.	...
Henfield	8 20	3 5	8 5	9 5	3 35	8 5	4 6	3 4	2 3	...
Steyning	8 30	3 15	8 15	9 15	3 45	8 15	3 3	2 6	1 8	...
Bramber	8 33	3 18	8 18	9 18	3 48	8 18	3 0	2 3	1 6	...
Shoreham	8 43	3 28	8 28	9 28	3 58	8 28	1 6	1 2	0 9	...
Kingston	8 48	3 33	8 33	9 33	4 3	8 33	1 3	1 0	0 8	...
Southwick	8 53	3 38	8 38	9 38	4 8	8 38	1 2	0 10	0 8	...
Portslade	8 56	3 41	8 41	9 41	4 11	8 41	1 0	0 9	0 6	...
Brighton (arrival)	9 5	3 50	8 50	9 50	4 20	8 50	...	...	...	...

GEO. HAWKINS,
Traffic Manager.

Brighton, June, 1861.

Fig.1.2 The public notice which announced the start of passenger services on the Steyning line after phase 1 had been completed. By courtesy of the late Eddie Collins, Curator of the former Bramber Museum.

The fourth reason was when a rural community, wishing to be connected to the rail net of the region of which it was a part, formed a company of its own. This would raise the money and arrange with a contractor for the line to be built. Before proceeding, of necessity, there had to be an agreement with the Company operating the main line with which it was desired that connection should be made. Agreements of this kind involved the larger company in leasing the branch from its principals at a fixed percentage of their capital outlay. Had its promoters not been short of a little under £8,000, it seems likely that the Steyning Company would have succeeded in building its line. Nevertheless, in the end, the "inhabitants of Steyning and District" enjoyed a better outcome than they had anticipated, for finally Mr. Lock's proposed line, which was another potential invasion of LBSCR territory, led to the construction by the LBSCR of a link between the Mid-Sussex line and the South Coast line at Shoreham-by-Sea.

What evidently counted strongly in its favour, when the two rival schemes were being considered by the House of Commons Committee, was the potential for a direct link between Brighton, West Sussex and Guildford which the LBSCR's proposed route would have been able to achieve.

Celebrating the Centenary of the Steyning line on 7th October 1961. An early LBSCR locomotive from Brighton Works, on a siding at Steyning station, is admired by children. *Author's collection.*

2 THE DEVELOPMENT OF THE REGIONAL RAIL NETWORK

The building of the Steyning line may be seen as part of an evolutionary process in the development of the rail network of South East England and in particular of West Sussex, East Hampshire and South West Surrey, shown in Fig 2.1. This process lasted over a period of nearly fifty years, from 1840, when the line between Shoreham and Brighton was opened, and 1887, the year in which the Dyke branch was brought into service.

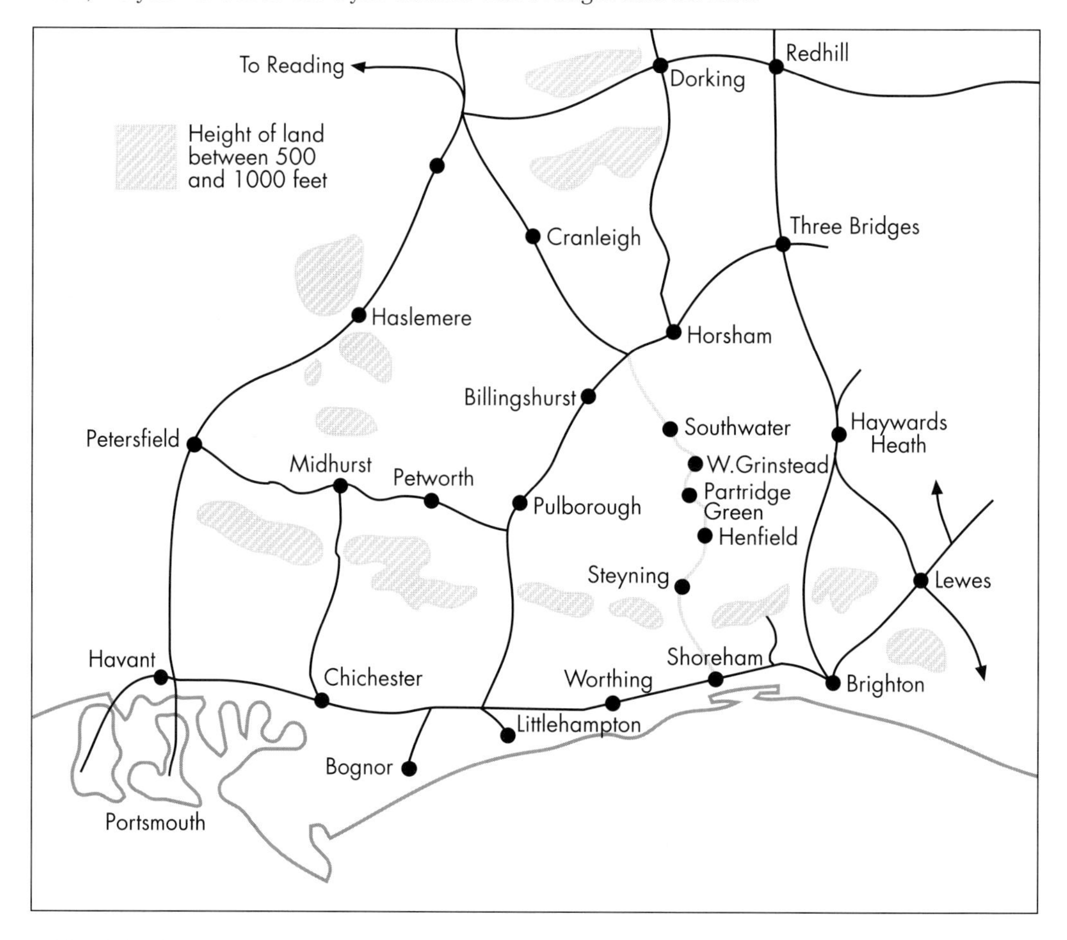

Fig 2.1 The railway network of West Sussex, East Hampshire and S.W. Surrey at its maximum extent circa 1930.

The complexity and density of the route pattern - omitting those parts of the network east of the Lewes-Redhill alignment - stemmed largely from the schemes of rival promoters. By the time they were brought together by grouping in 1922, to form part of the Southern Railway

Company, ownership of the constituent routes in the network had been reduced to three: the London and South Western Railway (LSWR), the South Eastern Railway (SER) and the London, Brighton and South Coast Railway (LBSCR), the latter having the lion's share of the local network.

There were three periods of constructional activity, each separated by almost a decade of quiescence. The evolution of the network may best be appreciated from the diagrammatic sketch maps in Figures 2.2 and 2.3 to which the reader may like to refer.

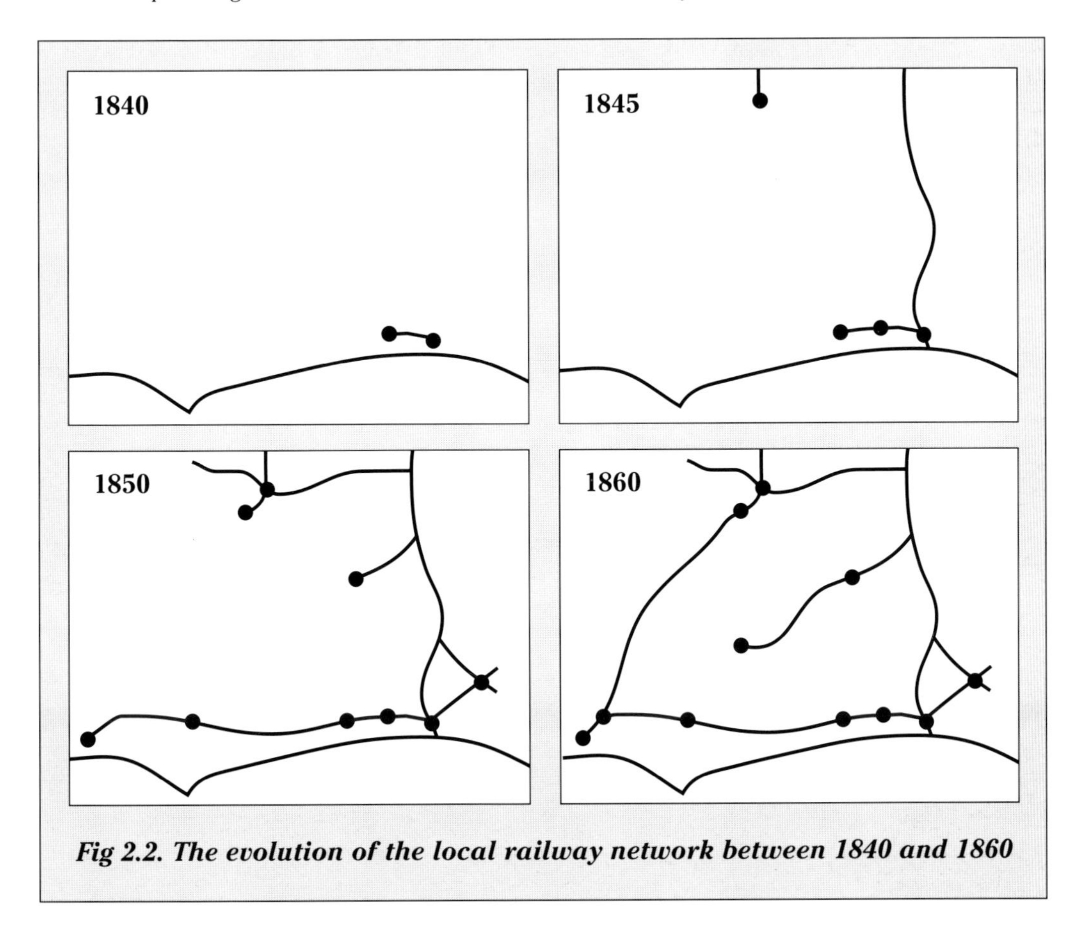

Fig 2.2. The evolution of the local railway network between 1840 and 1860

Fig 2.2 shows developments over the twenty years preceding the opening of the Steyning line. In 1840 the LBR opened the line from Shoreham into Brighton, thus making use of the port of Shoreham for bringing in materials and machinery for the main line which was completed and opened in the succeeding year. In 1845 the Brighton - Shoreham line was extended westward to Worthing and opened on 24th November while in the same year the London and South Western Railway opened their line from Woking to Guildford on the 5th May.

By the year 1850 the Coast line had been extended to Portsmouth, the links to Lewes from both Brighton and Wivelsfield completed, and a branch to Horsham from Three Bridges brought into use. In 1849 the LSWR had opened its line from Guildford to Godalming and the SER the line from Guildford to Ash and from Redhill to Shalford. This latter route was part of an alignment between Reading and Tonbridge, running powers being exercised between Shalford and Guildford over LSWR metals.

A major development in the following decade was the building by Thomas Brassey of the line from Godalming to a junction at Havant with the LBSCR's coast route to Portsmouth. It was now a question of which company would buy it from Brassey. In view of the low density of population of the country south of Godalming, through which Brassey's line passed, the LBSCR exercised caution and was not prepared to invest in it as large a sum as the two other contenders, of which one was the South Eastern Railway. That company, anticipating a successful bid, was sufficiently optimistic of an outcome in its favour as to build a spur south at Shalford; the earth formation for this, though never used, can still be seen. The outcome was that the LBSCR and SER were both beaten in their bids by the London and South Western Railway. Also included in this period was the opening on 10th October 1859, of the Mid-Sussex Company's line linking Horsham, Pulborough and Petworth. This, in due course, was acquired by the LBSCR.

Shoreham-by-Sea 'B' Box, level crossing and signals on 28th April 1969. The junction of the Steyning line is approximately half a mile ahead and the right-hand signal on the gantry controls entry of freight services to Beeding Cement Works, passenger services having been withdrawn three years earlier. *John Scrace.*

Fig. 2.3 shows continuing developments in the network. In 1861 the Steyning line was opened while construction was in progress from Hardham on the Horsham-Petworth line to connect with the Coast line south of Arundel. This became the well-used extension of the Mid-Sussex line, which came into service in 1863, serving Billingshurst, Pulborough, Amberley and Arundel. Branches to Littlehampton and Bognor were opened subsequently and in 1865 the Cranleigh line was completed between Horsham and Guildford, having been acquired by the LBSCR in the previous year.

During the next quinquennium, the most important development was the opening on 1st

May 1867, of the line from Leatherhead, south through Dorking, to Horsham, the route used latterly by express services between London Victoria, Bognor Regis and Portsmouth, connecting disparately at Horsham with most Steyning line services. Other lines opened were from Petworth to Midhurst (LBSCR), Petersfield to Midhurst (LSWR), Havant to Hayling Island (LBSCR), and a short branch to Kemp Town, Brighton off the Brighton to Lewes line.

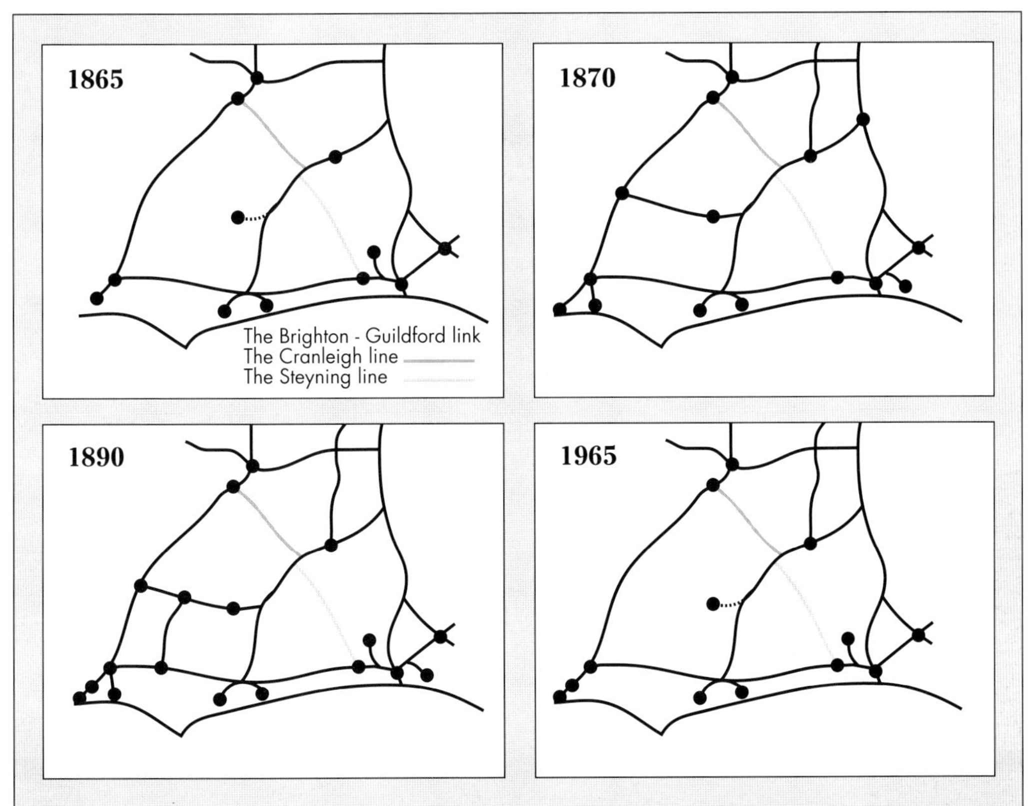

Fig 2.3 A century of evolution in the local network between 1865 and May, 1965. In June 1965 the Horsham - Guildford link, (the Cranleigh line) was closed.

The network was then nearly complete. After 1870, additions were small but important refinements. The first, in 1876, was a joint LBSCR-LSWR extension from Portsmouth Town to Portsmouth Harbour; the second, the construction of the Cliftonville spur between Hove and Preston Park. This was opened in 1879 and made possible the through running of trains between London and Worthing, without the necessity of their going into the terminus at Brighton where previously they had had to reverse. Two years later this was followed by the opening, on 11th July 1881, of a line between Chichester and Midhurst.

The network was completed in 1887 by two further developments. The first was the opening on 1st January of that year of a spur off the Littlehampton branch eastward, giving direct access to Littlehampton from Worthing. The second was that of the line up to Devil's Dyke, a famous beauty spot on the South Downs near Hove and Brighton. Apart from the closure in 1867 of the south fork from the Cranleigh line at Itchingfield, the network was to remain as it was built for almost another fifty years.

The Northern Extension of the Brighton - Guildford link, by the Horsham and Guildford Direct Railway Company

Opened on 2nd October 1865, just over four years after the completion of the Steyning line, this became the northern part of what had been intended to be the through rail link between Brighton and Guildford. Although, initially, the LBSCR directors were concerned that the promoters of the Horsham-Guildford scheme might sell out to the London and South Western Railway, which would then have access to territory they regarded as theirs, these concerns were met on 1st May 1860 by a communication they received from the promoters of the "Horsham and Guildford Direct Railway". In this the Brighton Company's Directors were asked if they would be "inclined to enter into an agreement to work the line when constructed". This, subject to appropriate conditions being met, they agreed to. By doing so, they would have seen a big financial saving in not having to extend their own line to Guildford through Billingshurst and Loxwood.

While there were delays in construction and protracted negotiations which largely involved access to Guildford Station over LSWR metals, LBSCR Directors were appointed to the H&G Board and Jacombe-Hood became, in a limited capacity, "Engineer-in-Chief". Although provision was made for a double line when constructing bridges and culverts, the line was otherwise single tracked with passing loops only at Cranleigh and Baynards Stations. With finances agreed, the LBSCR's influence increased to the point where a complete take-over by that Company was a logical outcome.

Overlooking, or perhaps not being aware that the promoters' original purpose had been to build a rail link between Horsham and Guildford, and obviously thinking of the Brighton connection, Jacombe-Hood surveyed and planned a spur leading south to join the Mid-Sussex line at Itchingfield, about one kilometre north of the junction with the Steyning line. After the Board had pointed out the omission of a junction towards Horsham, this too was duly surveyed and, with the Board's agreement, both spurs were built.

The photograph of Christ's Hospital station was taken on 15th October 1972. Subsequently it was demolished. *John Scrace.*

Christ's Hospital signal box 'A' photograph on 26th November 1967. Photo: *John Scrace.*

The completed single tracked railway linked what is now Christ's Hospital Station (opened at the end of the 19th Century) and Peasmarsh Junction on the LSWR's line to the south of Guildford. On the occasion of the opening, a special train from Horsham was run with senior officials of the Brighton Company on board and with festivities at stations along the route.

The potential the south spur at Itchingfield gave for running through trains from Brighton to Guildford and vice versa was not made use of by scheduled

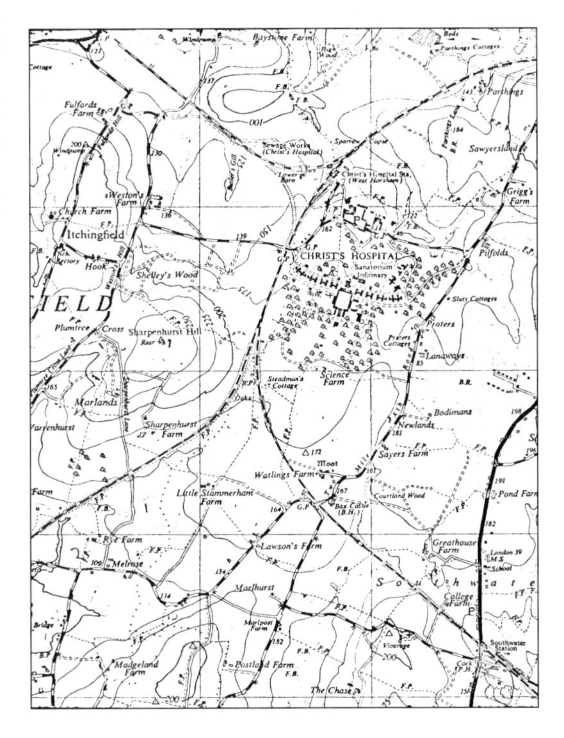

Fig 2.4 The embankment of the southern spur of the Cranleigh line was still existing in the year 1948 as can be seen from the O.S. map published in that year. The map extract also shows the line's north spur and junction at Christ's Hospital station together with the Steyning line from the south east joining the Mid-Sussex line at Itchingfield Junction.

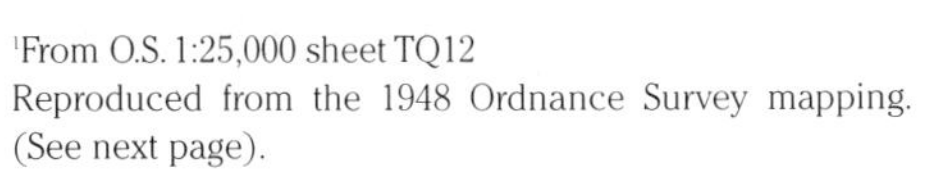
[1]From O.S. 1:25,000 sheet TQ12
Reproduced from the 1948 Ordnance Survey mapping. (See next page).

services and the track on the southern spur was removed in 1867. The main criterion in the thinking of LBSCR's management at that time was evidently to view the provision of a local service linking rural communities and the nearest main town as the reason for the line's existence. There may also have been continuing fears of a bid by the LSWR to take over the line and the southern spur might then have made possible an encroachment into LBSCR territory.

Up to the 1950s the low embankment forming the south spur continued to be a feature in the landscape, as is indicated in the 1:25,000 Ordnance Survey Map of that period[1]. Today, the embankment having now been removed and ploughed over, the former spur is marked by a shallow ditch which forms a field boundary, paralleled by a curved strip of coarse vegetation.

Conclusion

This chapter began with an examination of the way in which the various components of the local network, of which the Steyning line was a part, came together over a period of nearly fifty years after the first line in the area that between Shoreham and Brighton had been constructed, ending with a brief description of the Cranleigh line, an essential component if the intended provision of scheduled services between Brighton and Guildford was to be met. Reasons for this not having happened will be considered more fully in Chapter 3.

See No 87 of 'Locomotion Papers' for an excellent detailed description by H.R. Todd of the problems the Horsham to Guildford Direct Railway Company had in its early stages and subsequent history

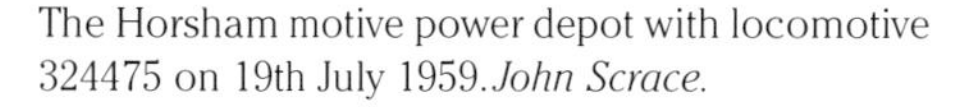

The Horsham motive power depot with locomotive 324475 on 19th July 1959. *John Scrace.*

3 THE HISTORICAL DIMENSION

Early days on the Line
Accidents
Value to the Farming Community
Industry
Value in War
The Post-war Context
Excursion Traffic
A Centenary Celebration
The Brighton - Guildford link
The Closure

Early Days on the Line

When the first phase of the Steyning line was completed, with three trains running daily between Brighton and Partridge Green THE WEST SUSSEX GAZETTE, of 4th July1861, carried a full description of the enterprise, including this comment:

"*...It is a well-constructed line, and those who are experienced in such matters, speak very highly of the manner in which Mr Firbank, the contractor, has done his work... Everything, we believe, is as perfect as can be desired; It was so pronounced by the government Inspector, Colonel Tyler, and there can be no doubt that the working of the line will be as complete as is the other part of the Brighton Railway Company's system.*"

A northbound train at Partridge Green. The original LBSCR buildings are on the "down" platform and date from when the Steyning line was single tracked. The signal box was a more recent construction of the late 19th century. *E. Wilmshurst.*

When the second phase was completed, the inauguration of services between Brighton and Horsham consisted of four stopping trains and one express daily. In 1867, the engine drivers on the line went on strike, asking that 10 hours a day or a run of 150 miles be reckoned a day's work. At that time, a driver earned a maximum of seven shillings and a fireman four shillings and sixpence for a day's work.

Although for the first eighteen years of its existence, the line was single tracked, a wise provision had been made at the outset by Jacombe-Hood, the Brighton line's Chief Engineer; this was for all bridges to be capable of taking two tracks. By the year 1878/9 traffic on the line had so grown, necessitating a greater frequency of trains, that the whole length of line between Shoreham-by-Sea and its confluence with the Mid-Sussex line at Itchingfield was doubled.

Accidents

The Steyning line was largely accident free. In its edition of 21 March 1861, The West Sussex Gazette reported how a youth carrying an eel spear was walking on the track well before the Line's opening, when a ballast train had come up behind him. Evidently the lad was deaf and did not hear the engine's whistle. He would have been run down but "the brake was applied and every means used to stop the train, fortunately with success."

In 1866 two passenger trains collided at Itchingfield Junction, resulting in one person being killed. It happened again in 1964, when engineering work on the Brighton main line made it necessary to send a freight train from Hove to Three Bridges via Steyning (this was almost routine at week-ends). On this occasion it seemed that diesel fumes had caused sleepiness in the engine's crew. After passing through Southwater the freight train passed a signal at danger and on reaching the junction at Itchingfield, the engine collided with a south-bound train on its way on the Mid-Sussex line from Three Bridges to Chichester. This resulted in the deaths of the two men in the freight train's driving cab.

An 'M7' 0-4-4 which would have spent most of its life on the South Western. This No. 30050 working the 09.30 Brighton - Horsham service approaching Horsham on 25th July 1959. *John Scrace.*

Except when during the Second World War a German bomb landed on the Mid-Sussex line south of Horsham and caused some discomfort to a freight train which ran into its crater, there were no other major incidents causing disruption to Steyning line services.

The Steyning Line's Value to the Farming Community

In peacetime as well as during the two world wars, the farming community in this rural area of West Sussex was immensely blessed by the existence of the line. After the line's opening, Steyning's weekly Market moved from the High Street of the ancient town to a field adjacent to the railway station and to and from it for over a century the railway transported cattle, sheep, poultry and many other items of produce for auction.

Before the railway came to Steyning, Jacombe-Hood, in his 1856 assessment of likely freight movement to Brighton's Market, listed *"grain, oil cake, stone and marble, coal, beer, barley, malt, hops, bricks, drapery and grocery goods, spirits, wood, flour, lime, stationery and fancy goods to an aggregate weight of 10,193 tons per annum. There would also at that time be approximately 300 'fat beasts' and 900 'fat sheep' sent annually to Brighton by road."*

"The total number of cattle now (in 1856) annually brought into Steyning fortnightly Market is about 26,643 - of these at least 9/10ths are seasonally sold and half of the number disposed of, which are principally purchased by the Brighton butchers, are now in the absence of Railway accommodation, driven wholly by road into Brighton for slaughter."

Jacombe-Hood's account of the cattle annually driven to Brighton from Steyning was:

Beast	949
Sheep	8941
Calves	423
Lambs	43
Pigs	441
	10,797

LBSCR Station Documents indicate a variety of goods brought to Steyning by rail in the late 19th Century, of which the following are examples from 1874 and 1875:

Year	
1874 From Littlehampton Goods:	10 sacks maize weighing 1 ton, 1 cwt
" From Brighton:	10 sacks of wheat weighing 1 ton.
1875 From Horsham:	14 bundles of timber weighing 4 cwt.
" From Lancing:	2500 bricks weighing 6 tons, 5 cwt.
" From Arundel:	One consignment cement weighing 3cwt.
" From Lancing:	5 tons of beach pebbles.

Mr. Jack Ash, a former Chairman of Steyning Parish Council and at the time of writing is Clerk to the Parish Council of Bramber, has described to the author how in his younger days he would act as drover for the Annual Sheep Fair at Findon, taking flocks of sheep over the Downs to Steyning from where they would be railed to their various destinations.

Milk traffic in 17-gallon churns was an important commercial item but it switched to road haulage at the time of the General Strike in 1926. With no trains to serve them or the general

Beeding Cement Works signal box. *E. Wilmshurst.*

The view south from Beeding signal box. The British Portland Cement works were located over to the left of the picture. *J E. Sleight.*

public, farmers then realised, instead of carting them to the nearest station, how much more convenient it was to load churns on to a lorry on their farm, to be conveyed direct to their destination. Subsequently, when the Strike was over, this continued and would have been one of many factors giving rise to a decline in the Railways' receipts. Similarly, in 1955, a national railway strike resulted in a severe reduction of freight traffic, particularly of coal which diverted to road, whilst a proportion of freight traffic continued to be transported off-rail afterwards. This contributed to British Rail closing goods yards on the Steyning line as elsewhere on the rail network.

Industry

While today there are industrial estates at Southwater and Partridge Green, these came into existence on former railway property after the line was closed. Long before that, two important industrial enterprises were the manufacture of fine quality bricks using Weald Clay at Southwater, and cement at Beeding, on the east flank of the River Adur. Input into the Cement Works consisted of clay piped as a slurry from Small Dole, chalk quarried at the site, Gypsum railed from Robertsbridge, and coal from Dover, while a once weekly trainload of cement was railed via Shoreham and the South Coast main line to the British Portland Cement depot at Southampton. The table will indicate to the reader the volume of this traffic in 1969 and 1970, which had continued after passenger services had been withdrawn. A single line continued in use between the Works and the South Coast main line until 1981.

SHOREHAM CEMENT WORKS - MOVEMENT OF WAGONS

← Rail Wagons into Works →					← Rail wagons out of Works →	
Year	Coal	Gypsum	General Stores	I	Cement	Flints
1951	5400	1140	100	I	9670	80
1960	7000	2300	100	I	7670	240
1969	5400	1730	20	I		150
1970		1850	20	I		220

Source: A personal communication to the author in 1972 from the General Manager, Associated Portland Cement, Shoreham Works.

After over 100 years of cement manufacture on that site, the Works finally closed in 1991.

Value In War

The value of the Guildford connection to the Steyning line was especially marked during the 1914-18 World War when, acting through the Railway Executive Committee, the Ministry of Transport assumed responsibility for all railway operations. Apart from normal services which would have been somewhat curtailed, many were the trains from Middle England which carried military equipment, ammunition and Service personnel bound for the Western Front via the Cranleigh and Steyning lines and the port of Newhaven. In the Second World War, from 1st September 1939, this function was repeated when both lines were an important supply route for the forces deployed in defence of the South Coast.

In June 1940, soon after the miracle of Dunkirk, when England was in imminent danger of invasion by German forces occupying France, General (later Field-Marshal) Bernard Montgomery had his Headquarters at Wiston House, located at the foot of the north-facing scarp of the South Downs near Steyning. Winston Churchill has described how:

"At the end of June, the Chiefs of Staff through General Ismay suggested to me at the Cabinet that I should visit the threatened sectors of the east and south coasts. Accordingly, I devoted a day or two every week to this agreeable task, sleeping when necessary in my train, where I had every facility for carrying on my regular work and was in constant contact with Whitehall.... One of my earliest visits was to the third division, commanded by General Montgomery (whose) Headquarters were near Steyning... I had very good talks with the General and enjoyed my outing thoroughly."[1]

From 1st August 1940, the First Division of the Canadian Army took over from the British 3rd Infantry Division the task of guarding the southern coastline. The Royal Canadian Mounted Police used Martin Lodge on Station Road at Henfield, and the Canadians' 1st Division had a large encampment close to the airfield at Shoreham and on the playing fields

Wiston House, Steyning, the Headquarters of General Montgomery in 1940. *Photo: John Bubb.*

[1] Winston S. Churchill. The Second World War Volume Two., (The Reprint Society (1953) p.220).

Troops on Steyning's station Road on a winter's day in 1915. *Courtesy of Steyning Museum.*

of Lancing College which had previously housed the Royal Ulster Rifles. For them, as for the British and Allied forces, the Cranleigh and Steyning lines were to play a vital role in transporting men, tanks and guns for the War's successful conclusion. These included the United States' Army movement of supplies during the year leading up to D-Day, including those from their encampment near Baynards at the southern end of the Cranleigh line.

The Post-war Context

Prior to the year 1948, four major railway companies served the whole of the United Kingdom. They had been formed by an Act of Parliament in the year 1922, amalgamating, by "grouping", some 120 independent enterprises into four regional companies. As the reader will recall, the Steyning and Cranleigh lines having previously been under the aegis of the London, Brighton and South Coast Railway, became part of the Southern Railway,

During the Second World War, as they had been in the First, the railways were operated by the Railway Executive Committee. They emerged from five and a half years of war in a seriously run down condition, having suffered severe losses of rolling stock by enemy action, virtually no track renewals, yet having operated over 500,000 trains for the war effort. Soon after the Japanese surrender in August 1945, the newly elected Government proposed that the nation's railway network be brought into public ownership. The "Big Four" continued to function until nationalisation took effect on 1st January 1948 with the establishment of another Railway Executive Committee. Matters were simplified much later when 'British Rail' came into being.

One disadvantage of public ownership was that revenues from taxation and the sale of Government Bonds, which might have been used to compensate the railways for their run-down condition, were in large measure used to buy all the shares of the four companies held by individuals and corporations. Without greatly increasing the national debt, the Treasury would understandably have been loathe to make money available for more than essential maintenance, let alone putting the railways back into their pre-war condition.

An example of this was the Southern Railway's scheme to electrify the Steyning line, for which some preliminary work had been done in the year before the onset of hostilities, when possible suitable sites for transformer sub-stations were investigated. On 31st October 1946, the Company announced their intention to proceed with the plan but soon after nationalisation took effect in January 1948, the scheme was abandoned presumably because of the cost involved and insufficient resources being made available from the Treasury.

On 30th April 1964 at Copsale, an Ivatt tank No. 41301 hauls the 15.21 train from Horsham bound for Brighton. The high quality of the track is evident in this rural stretch north of West Grinstead. *John Scrace.*

Track maintenance continued to be at a high standard as demonstrated by a report in The Shoreham Herald of 26th July 1957:

"For the second time in four years a Steyning permanent way gang have won the award for the most improved length of class C track in the Brighton district of British Railways..."

The men who worked on the line between Steyning and Henfield received their award from Mr J. Parker, Southern Region District Engineer at Steyning Station.

One of the Gang, Mr Herman Ramm had been a prisoner of war in England during the 1939-45 conflict. He returned to settle in England after the war because he *"liked the country so much"*.

On right lines with their line

The Steyning Permanent Way Gang (Left to right): F. Knight, R. Hyder, M.W. Matthews, M.Ramm and W.J. Smith. M.Woolgar, not in the photograph, was on holiday. *Photo' Shoreham Herald.*

Excursion Traffic

From the Steyning line's inception, in addition to normal daily operations, excursions proved immensely popular, starting with one to Portsmouth in July 1861, soon after the line up to Partridge Green had been opened. The fare charged was two shillings and 185 persons took advantage of it. Then, in August 1861, there was an excursion via Hove to Crystal Palace.

In the 20th century, a characteristic of summer weekend traffic in peacetime was of through running of excursions to Brighton and Hove from Wolverhampton, Banbury, Oxford and Reading, via Guildford and Horsham. And during the autumn and winter, when Brighton and Hove Albion were playing on their home ground, there would inevitably be "Specials" to Hove from Guildford, Horsham and further north. These trains would usually consist of eight or ten carriages hauled in latter years by a West Country or Battle of Britain Class Pacific. A typical excursion from London in Southern Railway days is shown in the promotion leaflet illustrated in Fig 3.1.

The general public's use of the Steyning line will be examined by referring to station records in Chapter 4.

A Battle of Britain 4-6-2 Pacific No. 340500 'Royal Observer Corps' hauling an LGB excursion from East Sussex is approaching Bramber from the South and will shortly arrive at Steyning. *E. Wilmshurst.*

A Centenary Celebration

On the initiative of senior boys attending Steyning Grammar School, the centenary of the completion of phase two and inauguration of the route between Brighton and Horsham was celebrated on Saturday, 7th October 1961. An exhibition was held in the waiting room at Steyning Station, the signal box and station were decorated with bunting and trains carried headboards marking the occasion.

The through connection between Brighton and Guildford

With one or two exceptions the interchange facility for passengers changing from a Steyning line to a Cranleigh line train, usually involved a tiresome wait. As the reader will see from the table on the next page, the reason for this lay in the timetable connections - or the lack of them - at Christ's Hospital and at Horsham. The deficiency can be explained in part by the Cranleigh line, from its inception, having remained single tracked for the greater part of its length. This undoubtedly inhibited integration of train schedules with those of the Steyning line. If there had been adequate finance in the post-war period, doubling the tracks should have solved this problem. Better still would have been restoration of the track on the south spur, making some fast, or semi-fast through services a feasible option. It seems that rail managers treated the Cranleigh line as a backwater; understandable if its potential was not fully realised, added to the previous state of the nation's economics at that time.

THE BRIGHTON - GUILDFORD LINK

Mon - Sat Connections at Christ's Hospital Station and Horsham
(No service between Horsham and Guildford on Sundays)

				Sats. only			Not Sats.
Brighton dep.		06.25	11.28	14.28	15.28	16.29	18.13
C. Hospital arr.		07.22	12.16	15.17	16.16	17.20	19.04
Horsham arr.		07.28	12.21	15.22	16.21	17.25	19.09
Horsham dep.	06.46	07.55	12.09	15.09	16.53	18.15	19.09
C. Hospital	06.52	08.00F	12.18	15.19A	16.59	18.24	19.20
Guildford	07.35	08.42	13.06B	16.06	17.45C	19.10D	20.15E

A. arr C.H. 6 minutes earlier
B waited at Cranleigh 10 minutes
C " " 5 minutes and at Bramley 3 minutes
D " " 9 minutes
E " " 13 minutes
F at C.H. 1 minute earlier & dep 2 mins later on Saturdays

				Sats. only			Not Sats.
Guildford dep.	08.04	10.34	13.14	17.04	18.05	19.34	20.34
C. Hospital dep.	08.50F	11.14H	14.18	17.45	18.55	20.13	21.21G
Horsham arr.	08.54	11.18I	14.22	17.50	19.00	20.18	21.26
Horsham dep	09.30	11.30	14.30	18.33	19.30	20.30	21.25
C. Hospital dep.	09.34	11.34	14.34	18.37	19.34	20.34	21.29
Brighton arr.	10.24	12.24	15.34	19.27	20.24	21/24	22.17

F waited at Cranleigh 5 minutes
G waited at Baynards 5 minutes
H waited at Christ's Hosp 6 minutes on Saturdays.
I arr. Horsham at 11.24 on Saturdays.
Steyning line (Brighton-Horsham) trains ran hourly. Only those which connected with trains to and from Guildford are shown in the table.

SOURCE: The 1964-65 British Rail Timetable for Southern Region

In 1961 A Centenary special is passing the sidings of Beeding Cement Works. Photo: *E. Wilmshurst.*

Celebrating the Steyning line's centenary (1861-1961) is the 15.19 Horsham to Brighton service at Christ's Hospital hauled by a former LSWR M7 0.4.4 tank just arriving at Christ's Hospital. The platform for Guildford line services is just visible to the left of the signal box. *John Scrace.*

The Closure

The last steam service is well described in Philip Barnes' *'The Steyning Line Rail Tour'*. After eighteen months of diesel working, passenger services were finally withdrawn with the last train from Brighton to Horsham on the evening of Sunday 6th March 1966.

The West Sussex Gazette of 10th February 1966 reported:

"A meeting between the Railways Board and the Ministry of Transport last Wednesday seemed certain to result in putting off yet again the fateful deed, but a firm decision to go ahead with the closure came in the late afternoon... So rings down the curtain on a service that undoubtedly was "borderline" if it should be closed or not. Certainly those who used the line regularly fought hard enough to save it, and even the Railways Board admitted to many misgivings as to whether their decision was the right one in all the circumstances."

In the following week, a train of wagons went up the line to take on board furniture and fittings from all the stations and outbuildings. These were off-loaded at Christ's Hospital and stacked on the already redundant platform which had served the Guildford line. In the week after that, demolition of the track began.

Mr Jack Burt who was in charge of the operation, describes how British Rail, perhaps because of the public outcry and opposition to the closure, lost no time in lifting the most recently laid flat-bottomed rails which were in first class condition. The work went on seven days a week until that part of the operation was complete. A contractor was then employed in the following Autumn to lift the remainder.

Signal boxes were the first railway buildings to be demolished, with stations going the same way in 1969. Goods traffic from Shoreham Cement Works continued on a single track down to Shoreham for another fourteen years until it too was closed.

The ensuing chapters will introduce to the reader the reasoning which gave rise to the Steyning line's closure. In the light of this reasoning, interest may focus on levels of traffic which will be presented.

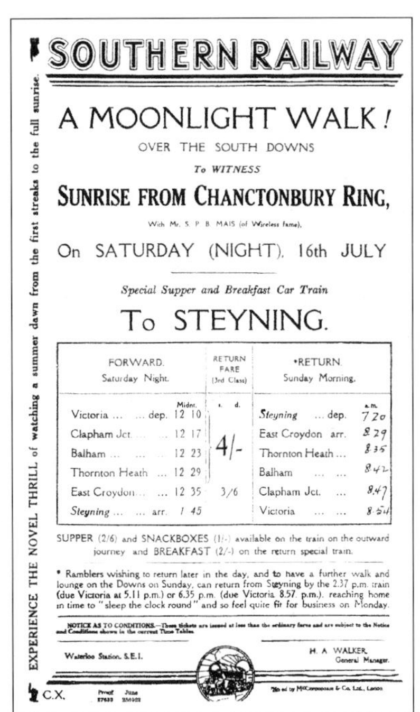

Fig 3.1 A typical excursion promotion leaflet which would have been available at stations in the London area.

April 1972 - six years after the withdrawal of passenger services the single Up line connects the cement works at Beeding with the South coast main line at Shoreham. *Photo: Author.*

Six years after the line's closure and all the track north of Beeding lifted, the fortnightly cattle market at Steyning continued but road transport had to be used. The cattle bay at Steyning station no longer in use shows dereliction. *Photo: Author.*

April 1972 - six years after passenger services had been withdrawn, the Beeding Cement Works were still a hive of industry. *Photo: Author.*

Part of the track layout at Beeding Cement Works. The former Up line is on the left of the picture. *Photo: Author.*

4 BRITISH RAIL'S CENSUS OF 1962-64

Testing usage in general
Application between Brighton and Horsham
Additional census with diesel /electric traction
Perceptions of declining traffic
A long-term statistical base

Testing the Public's use of the line

The story of the line moves on from the immediate post-war period to 1962. In that year, the services on the whole of Britain's railway network came under close scrutiny. This involved investigating how many people actually used the services provided and was undertaken during weeks when the number of passengers could be regarded as typical of what was happening under summer and winter conditions.

The process involved a nation-wide census, when the numbers of passengers joining and alighting from trains were counted in the course of sample weeks in three consecutive years.

For Steyning line services, one series of counts was held over seven days in November 1962 and a second under summer conditions in July 1963. For Sunday traffic in that year, a sample was taken during the month of August. In addition to those on the Steyning line itself,

A late summer afternoon. Passengers on the "up" platform eagerly await the arrival of their train from Brighton which can be just seen emerging from the cutting south of the station. *Photo: Author's collection.*

during each of the test weeks checks were made at each station on the main coast line between Brighton and Shoreham and also at Christ's Hospital and Horsham on the Mid-Sussex line.The input from both these sectors is reflected in the totals of passenger loadings. The results, which were issued by the railway authorities, give Monday to Friday figures as arithmetic means (daily averages), while those for the two Saturdays and Sundays are actual measures. The choice of week for each count suggests there was a satisfactory sampling of traffic to allow for seasonal adjustments. The reader will find the census counts' data for Steyning line services detailed below. It is perhaps significant that the two counts of people boarding and alighting from trains at weekends in summer and winter show strong similarity. To avoid bemusing my readers with a mass of statistics involving returns for each station on every day of the test weeks, the summary table below is an otherwise accurate record of the use made of the line by the travelling public.

PASSENGER LOADINGS BETWEEN SHOREHAM & CHRIST'S HOSPITAL

	November 1962 Averages		July 1963 Averages		November 1964 Averages
	Daily	Weekly	Daily	Weekly	Daily (Mon-Fri)
UP	1,000		1,020		921
DOWN	1,002		962		924
Totals	2,002 x 5 =	10,010	1,982 x 5 =	9,910	1,845 x 5 = 9,225*
Sats actual UP		879		822	
Sats actual Down		869		830	
Sunday actual Up		402		524	
Sunday actual Down		455		563	
Weekly average totals:		12,615		12,649	

* *With the omission of schools' traffic, reduced by approximately 1,000.*

About to depart for Horsham but first taking water on Steyning stations "up" platform. *Photo: M.S. Loader*

Diesel Traction takes over from Steam

In June 1964 there was a change from steam to diesel traction and because a decision was pending concerning the future operation of the line a further census of traffic on Steyning line trains was held in November of that year. It should be noted that this further count was concerned only with the numbers of passengers using Monday to Friday services and for that reason there is for that year no data for Saturday and Sunday working.

While on some trains there was virtually no change on others, while not reflected in the final total, *the census counts of 1964 showed a modest decrease in some passenger loadings compared with the 1963 figures* although an important element, that of school traffic, had been eliminated by choosing in that year the first week in November. As in the year 2001, this coincided with the schools' half-term break. The arithmetic mean of the number of people boarding and alighting from one and possibly two trains in each direction daily in that week was therefore reduced by approximately 200 and by 1,000 for the whole Monday to Friday period. If those numbers had been included for the Monday to Friday period, the 1964 total would have been above that of 1962.

Unit 1113 10.30 Horsham - Brighton at Horsham 10th October 1965. *Photo: John Scrace.*

When the Railways' Board obtained the Minister's consent to their proposal to withdraw passenger services from the Steyning line, they retained discretion whether or not to defer a decision as to the line's future or to proceed with closure. It is on record, referred to in the previous chapter, that officials debating the issue came down in favour of closure partly, it must be presumed, on account of a perceived loss of traffic indicated by a decline in season ticket sales but also by the misleading statistic yielded by the census of November 1964 which omitted normal school traffic.

An Ivatt tank No. 41301 hauls the 13.30 Brighton to Horsham train leaving West Grinstead on 30th April 1964. The photograph shows part of the track layout just to the north of the station. The non-passenger traffic from West Grinstead consisted of horse boxes serving nearby racing stables. *John Scrace.*

The real bone of contention in officials' minds seems to have concerned monthly and quarterly season tickets issued, because in other respects, judged from the records of tickets sold and handed in, detailed in Chapter 5, traffic on the line appears to have been increasing.

The year 1948 saw 993 quarterly and other long term season tickets issued; by 1959 the number had increased to 1,628 but thereafter underwent a decline until, in 1965, the number sold to the public had dropped to 1,215. This decline could partly be explained by the threat of closure, which had been made in the summer of 1963, as a result of which members of the public would not unreasonably have made contingency provision; partly by the poor connections of branch and main-line trains at Horsham, to which the reader will find a more detailed reference is given in Chapter 8; but also by an increasing number of people working a five day week. For them, using cheap-day returns from Monday to Friday was less expensive than buying weekly or longer term season tickets.

Records of stations' monthly returns give details of the number of weekly season tickets issued on the line, from 694 in 1948, peaking at 955 in 1964 but making a modest decline to 890 in 1965.

Overall, this has been a sample picture. While the logistics of traffic revealed by census counts would appear to have favoured a "wait and see" policy regarding the line's future, the reader might justly wonder whether slight reductions in the census counts from one year to another were short-term fluctuations or long-term trends. Clarification of this would depend on a long-term statistical base being available but which appears to have been overlooked by the Railways' Board in determining policy. This statistical base was available in the form of monthly returns of tickets sold and collected at each station, of which no mention was made at the Public Inquiry.

A long-term statistical base

After examining the data provided by the six census counts detailed above, the reader will find it possible to assess the longer-term trends of passenger use, made possible by analysing the monthly returns which were sent in from each station on the Steyning line to the Southern Region's Central Division Headquarters at Croydon. For the Steyning line, these records, as detailed in the next chapter, covered the whole eighteen year period from 1948 until March 1966 when passenger services were withdrawn.

Partridge Green locomotive 41287, a typical Ivatt 2-6-2 tank heads the 13.21 ex Horsham to Brighton train on its way to the next stop, Henfield on 22nd April 1964. *John Scrace.*

5 PASSENGER TRAFFIC IN THE POST-WAR PERIOD - 1948 TO 1965

Station Records on British Rail's Southern Region
The Station Records for the Steyning Line Examined
Notional Weekly Averages of Journeys
Census and Notional Weekly Averages Compared
Discussion of Trends of Traffic
Conclusion

In Chapter 4 the need was seen for a long-term statistical base which might give some indication of traffic trends. To create such a base, investigation of ticket sales which took place on the branch over a period of eighteen years and two months, from January 1948 to the last day of February 1966, yielded some significant data. Because it is more convenient to consider whole years, while the January and February 1966 records are set forth on their own, examination of the statistics will be taken up to December 1965. This will involve an analysis of ticket sales and a development of a method by which census data examined in Chapter 4 may be related to them.

From annual totals of tickets collected and of dockets and season tickets issued, the reader will be able to derive a notional picture of weekly traffic. Because of insufficiency of detail, this will be treated as "notional". By comparing the known passenger statistics examined in Chapter 4 with the notional assessment of weekly traffic for the same period of time, the derived figure will be used as a correcting factor for all weekly notional values when there were no census counts. Thus, it will be possible to determine an *assumed weekly average* for each year from 1948 to 1965. This will provide a quantitive picture of traffic throughout the eighteen years of the line's operation under the aegis of British Rail. Apart from this an examination of station records alone will yield an indication of trends at least as precise as the records may be presumed to have been accurate. A reason for wishing to extend our knowledge in this way, is in order that the reader may be better able to assess the policy of closure as it affected part of the railway network of the South East in the particular case of the Steyning line.

Station Records on the Southern Region of British Rail

In a personal communication in 1971, Mr P.W.Glassblower, Economic Survey officer for the Southern Region, referred to the fact that over the whole of British Railway's network "... *nationalisation and the cessation of clearing meant there were only global accounts.*"

Before nationalisation, "clearing" meant that when a person bought a through ticket to travel on the lines of different railway companies, the Railway Clearing House in London distributed the revenue to each company involved in proportion to the distance travelled by that person on the different companies' lines.

The reader might infer from the "cessation of clearing" that, after the railways of the United Kingdom were nationalised in 1947, until Dr Beeching became Chairman of the Railways Board in 1962, the economic viability of individual parts of the network were not regarded as important in determining future policy. Nevertheless, on British Rail's Southern Region at

The 12.19 ex Horsham to Brighton just south of the level crossing and Toll Bridge at Old Shoreham hauled by an Ivatt 2-6-2 tank not long before steam was replaced by diesel electric units in 1964. *E. Wilmshurst.*

least, a long established procedure was continued. This was for each station in the Region to submit to the appropriate Line Manager a return *at monthly intervals* of all business conducted.

The Steyning line was part of the Central Division of British Rail's Southern Region, in the Headquarters of which at Essex House, East Croydon, information relating to the line was available for as far back as records were held, that is from 1948 up to the time the line was closed in the year 1966.

The Station Records Examined

Passenger tickets issued.

Table 5.1 on the next page shows that the total number of tickets issued at branch stations in the year 1948 was 58,086. The number increased in 1949 but in 1950 they fell to 54,403.

Thereafter a rising trend in sales was resumed. By the year 1960, the numbers of tickets issued had more than doubled. These figures suggest there was a marked increase in passenger traffic on the branch in the post-1950 period, with a particularly strong rise in the quinquennium 1955-1960. During the first part of this period, from 1951 to 1954, the annual increase was almost constant and in 1954 was about 20,000 tickets above the 1950 figure.

A negative fluctuation in 1955 was succeeded in 1956 by a recovery so that ticket sales in that year were slightly above the previous maximum in 1954. There then followed, in the year 1957, an increase in the sales of tickets larger than the total increase between the years 1950 - 54. Over the succeeding three years this trend continued. The peak year for ticket sales was 1960; thereafter, until 1964, sales declined. The total decrease for these four years, however, was roughly half the increase which had been recorded over the two years from 1958 to 1960. In 1965 a positive trend appears to have been re-established to an extent that completely recovered the decline of the previous two years; nevertheless, in March 1966, the officials mentioned at the end of Chapter 3, possibly unaware of these trends, decided that the line should be closed.

STATISTICS OF PASSENGER TICKETS ISSUED AND COLLECTED AT STEYNING LINE STATIONS

Year	Tickets Sold	Tickets Collected	Year	Tickets Sold	Tickets Collected
1948	58,086	90,076	1957	99,134	110,793
1949	60,087	78,563	1958	106,110	126,272
1950	54,403	73,510	1959	118,995	150,427
1951	57,146	73,443	1960	125,293	145,936
1952	63,816	86,745	1961	122,151	140,049
1953	69,311	92,285	1962	119,970	133,616
1954	74,026	91,358	1963	116,919	135,225
1955	72,682	90,435	1964	115,057	137,189
1956	75,364	96,366	1965	120,016	140,129

Table 5.1 showing tickets sold and collected at Steyning line stations over the 18 year period from 1948 to 1965

Tickets collected

Fig 5.1 shows that the numbers of tickets collected followed trends similar to those of tickets issued. The quantity was greater, the reason for this being that in addition to return halves of tickets previously issued on the line, there would have been outward portions of tickets or single tickets purchased elsewhere on British Rail's network. For this reason, the "returns" of tickets collected will be used for gaining an understanding of traffic levels over the 18 years from January 1948 to December 1965. The reader will see by inspection of Fig 5.1 that the peak was attained in the year 1959, whereas, for ticket sales, the peak year was 1960.

Three elements for creating a statistical model, using "Tickets Returned" as core values, are:

1. The return halves of "cheap day" and "monthly" return tickets with outward portions of return and single tickets issued at another branch station or elsewhere.

2. Excess fare dockets issued

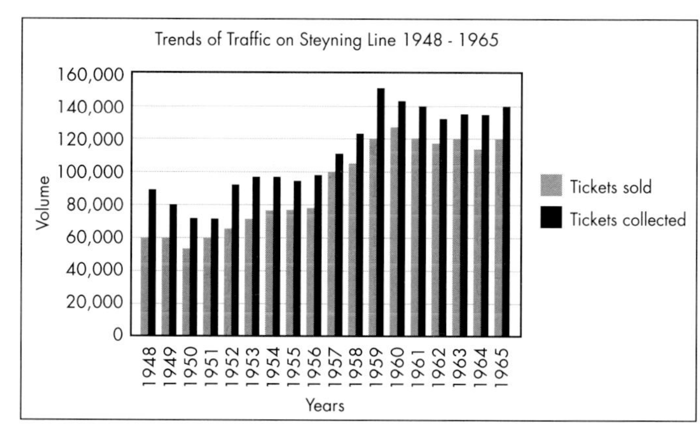

Fig 5.1 Showing proportions of tickets sold and collected.

on the branch.

3 Season tickets issued on the branch.

Although as an indicator of traffic trends, this set of data is marginally more effective than the statistics of "Tickets Issued", it does not include single journey tickets issued on the branch for destinations elsewhere on the railway network, nor does it include throughput which involved passengers "in transit" from one primary route sector to the other, examples of which will be given in the next chapter. A question which may occur to the reader is whether the financial input these gave to the system would have entered into the financial assessment of the Steyning line's viability. With the former railway companies' system of "clearing" having been abandoned, it is more likely that this element would have been credited to the line on which the ticket purchase had been made.

Cost advantage concerning tickets and dockets

The table below shows the number of tickets and dockets issued between 1961 and 1965 at Steyning line stations.

Years >>	1961	1962	1963	1964	1965
No of tickets collected ('T' values)	140,049	133,616	135,225	132,189	140,129
Excess fare dockets issued ('E' values)	3,532	4,309	4,490	3,958	3,521
Weekly season tickets issued ('W' values)	907	668	856	955	890
Quarterly season tickets ('Q' values)	1,536	1,523	1,415	1,394	1,215

Table 5.2 Tickets and dockets issued and collected over the last five complete years before passenger services were withdrawn.

Since return tickets are less expensive than buying two singles for a round trip, the author assumes that 85% of tickets handed in at stations were homeward portions of return tickets issued on the Steyning line itself and 15% were either "singles" or outward portions of return tickets issued elsewhere on the rail network. Each homeward portion of a return ticket thus represents two journeys. An estimate of the number of journeys these tickets represent involves simply doubling 85% of the numbers issued.

Of return tickets collected some would have been excess fare dockets; the proportion of return journeys these represented is likely to have been lower, and at a guess 60%, while 40% would have been for single journeys.

If the total number of tickets handed in at Steyning line stations is represented by 'T' and the number of excess fare dockets by 'E', then, each year, the number of journeys 'N' they represent, may be computed from:

$$N = 2(0.85\,T) + 0.15\,T = 1.70\,T + 0.15\,T = 1.85\,T$$

and

$$N = 2(0.60\,E) + 0.40\,E = 1.20\,E + 0.40\,E = 1.60\,E$$

The Shoreham Toll Bridge and signal box. Photo: *E. Wilmshurst.*

The results of the computation are entered in Table 5.3. for the last five years of the Steyning line's operation and in Table 5.4 for all eighteen years from 1948 to 1965.

Season Tickets

These can be treated similarly. When, for each year, there was a return made of Weekly (W) and Quarterly (Q) season tickets issued, it may be assumed that for each week the season ticket covered six days on which journeys were made. These would have represented six returns, or twelve journeys for the week. Computation of the weekly journeys made in the quinquennium covering the census years dealt with in Chapter 4, would then yield data as follows:

A. For weekly seasons, the number of journeys (N) made in a year is the product of the number of weekly seasons (W) issued and the journeys made in each week which would have been twelve in number. Thus, N = 12W.

B. For quarterly seasons, since there are 13 weeks in each quarter, this works out as N = 13 x 6 x 2 = 156 journeys for each of these tickets issued (where 13 stands for the number of weeks in each quarter, 6 the number of days travel in a week and 2 the number of daily journeys). The final result for N in this case is 156Q.

For each year in the quinquennium, the total number of journeys derived from the number of tickets which were returned and in the case of season tickets the numbers issued, are all listed in Table 5.3 and for all 18 years before passenger services were withdrawn, in Table 5.4.

The significance of revealed trends

The numbers of ordinary tickets issued and collected on the Steyning line from 1948 to

1965 indicate that traffic on the line on that account increased substantially.

Also, although the number of weekly season tickets issued fluctuated from year to year, there was, in the long term, an overall increase. Up to the year 1959, these components of the total traffic on the line were added to by an increase which also occurred in the number of people who travelled on quarterly or other long term season tickets; thereafter these went into decline so that the overall total of traffic in 1965 was some 2,000 passengers fewer each week than had travelled in 1959. Whereas in 1959 the *assumed weekly traffic* was a little in excess of 14,400, in 1965 it was reduced to little more than 12,250.

Although the decline in traffic after 1959 would obviously have been a cause for concern, it was not without precedent. From 1948 to 1950, there had been an even greater decline, amounting in that two year period to an apparent loss of traffic of 2,500 passengers each week, the later fall involved a loss of a smaller number of people over a longer period of time.

What is of greater significance is the magnitude of the increase of traffic from 1950 to 1959. This increase resulted in traffic in the latter year being more than double the 1950 volume. Even after the decline of the previous five years, the 1965 figure was only 100 passengers short of twice the 1950 figure.

Two comments on the decline in the use of season tickets

Following the publication of the Beeching Report in July 1963, once the Railways' Board had made known their intention to seek the Minister of Transport's consent for them to withdraw passenger services from the Steyning line, many people would have begun to make provision for their future transport needs. It is not surprising that there was then a decline in the number of quarterly season tickets sold, from 1415 in 1963 to 1215 in 1965. However, there is another factor to be taken into account. By that time, day returns had become a major component in commuter traffic. With five day working weeks fast becoming the established norm for people who did not commute to London, as will be made clear in a later chapter, it was less expensive to travel on cheap day return tickets rather than in purchasing monthly or quarterly "seasons", which people would not, as formerly, have needed at weekends. Nevertheless it was largely the decline in season ticket sales that British Rail officials, supported by the Ministry of Transport, based their argument for closure on their perception that traffic was falling. However, by the time passenger services were withdrawn in March 1966, the year 1965 had seen use of the line by people buying tickets and by those who arrived at stations on the branch from elsewhere was on an upward trend.

Notional Weekly Averages of Journeys

A "notional" figure for journeys each year may be taken as the sum of all journeys covered by the various kinds of ticket referred to above. By totalling all the annual journeys accounted for by these four items it will be possible to arrive at a figure which, divided by 52, will be a weekly assessment of traffic, differing from the true average for any given year by the amount of traffic which was throughput and unknown errors inevitably arising from the nature of these calculations. There is a need, therefore, of finding some way of introducing a correcting factor which will bring the notional weekly averages closer to an approximation of the true weekly averages. A method by which this may be achieved is simply to compare notional weekly averages over a given time span with precise statistical data from another source. This requirement is fulfilled by the availability of British Rail's census data of 1962-63, and will be considered below.

The criteria laid down earlier in this chapter for determining the Notional Weekly Average for any one year is expressed by: $N = \frac{1.85\,T + 1.60\,E + 12\,W + 156Q}{52}$

Early evening in early March at Partridge Green. *John Scrace.*

Applying this formula, the NWA for each of the last five years of the line's operation can be calculated as set out in the following table (Table 5.3).

Year >>	1961	1962	1963	1964	1965
1.85 T becomes for each year	259,091	247,190	250,166	244,550	259,239
1.60 E	5,651	6,894	7,184	6,333	5,634
12 W	10,884	8,016	10,272	11,460	10,680
156 Q	239,616	237,588	220,740	217,464	189,540
Annual totals of journeys -	515,242	499,688	488,362	479,807	465,093
A notional weekly average (NWA) will be 1/52 of annual total	9,909	9,609	9,392	9,227	8,944

Table 5.3 Shows the derivation of a notional weekly average (NWA) of passenger use for the last five years of the line's operation.

Census and Notional Weekly Averages Compared.

Referring back to matters dealt with in Chapter 4, the census weeks' mean for 1962 and 1963 (but not 1964 because no Saturday and Sunday counts were made in that year), is as follows: Nov 1962 / July 1963

Average weekly totals for two census weeks: (12,615 + 12,649) ÷2 = 12,632

If the Census weeks' mean of 12,839 is divided by the mean of NWA for the five years from

Year	1948	1949	1950	1951	1952	1953	1954	1955	1956	1957	1958	1959	1960	1961	1962	1963	1964	1965
T values	90076	78563	73510	73443	86745	92285	91358	90435	96366	110793	126272	150427	145936	140049	133616	135225	132189	140129
E values	2046	1873	1719	1995	1933	2310	2409	2169	2176	2510	2991	3566	3835	3532	4309	4490	3958	3521
W values	694	440	239	279	450	390	508	257	288	475	547	843	604	907	668	856	955	890
Q values	993	1007	1020	986	1021	1135	1090	1134	1210	1485	1477	1628	1462	1536	1523	1415	1394	1215
1.85 T	166641	145342	135994	135869	160478	170727	169012	167305	178277	204967	233603	278290	269982	259091	247190	250166	244550	259239
1.60 E	3273	2997	2750	3192	3093	3696	3854	3470	3482	4016	4786	5706	6136	5651	6894	7184	6333	5634
12 W	8328	5280	2868	3348	5400	4680	6096	3084	3456	5700	6564	10116	7248	10884	8016	10272	11460	10680
156 Q	154908	157092	159120	153816	159276	177060	170040	176904	188760	231660	230412	253968	228072	239616	237588	220740	217464	189540
Annual Totals	333151	310711	300732	296226	328247	356163	349002	350763	373975	446343	475365	548080	511438	515242	499688	488362	479807	465093
1/52 of Annual Totals (Nml Wkly Av)	6407	5975	5783	5697	6312	6849	6711	6745	7192	8583	9142	10540	9835	9909	9609	9392	9227	8944
1.34 NWA=AWA	8598	8018	7761	7645	8471	9191	9006	9052	9652	11518	12269	14145	13199	13298	12895	12604	12383	12003

TABLE 5.4 TRAFFIC IN THE PRE-CLOSURE PERIOD

Source: T, E, W and Q values from Traffic Records, Central Division of British Rail's Southern Region

Statistics for T, E, W and Q values over the full eighteen years of the line's operation between 1948 and 1965. T values refers to ordinary tickets handed in at Steyning line stations. These would have been "return halves" of tickets issued on the line or outward portions plus single tickets issued elsewhere on British Rail network (see Figure 5.1). E values refer to the average weekly number of journeys represented by excess fare dockets. W values refer to average weekly journeys represented by weekly season tickets issued. Q values refers to average weekly journeys represented by quarterly season tickets. NWA stands for Notional Weekly Average. AWA stands for Assumed Weekly Average.

1961 to 1965, a possible correcting factor for all eighteen years will be available.

The mean of the notional weekly totals set out in Table 5.3, including the two census years, is given by: (9,909 + 9,609 + 9,392 + 9,227 + 8,944) ÷5 yields an average of 9,416 journeys. A possible correcting factor will then be $\frac{12,632}{9,416} = 1.34$.

This is the correcting factor which will now be used for determining another set of values which will be called "Assumed Weekly Averages" (AWA), approximating to true weekly averages over the eighteen years from 1948 to 1965, shown in the bottom line of Table 5.4.

Determining "assumed weekly averages" (AWA)

The assumed weekly average of traffic on the Steyning line indicated in Table 5.4 for all the years 1948 to 1965 has been obtained from the product of 1.34 and the average notional weekly number of journeys for any given year. As a comparison with the census figures of 1962 and 1963, the AWA for each of those two years was

Census Figure	AWA
1962 (12,615)	12,895
1963 (12,649)	12,604

It will be seen that the assumed weekly averages for the years 1962 and 1963 are not greatly different from those two years' census counts.

Tourist Attractions

Earlier in this chapter, one of the reasons for the difference in the numbers of tickets sold and collected was referred to. The reader will see from Table 5.1 that in 1965, the year before Steyning line passenger services were withdrawn, this difference amounted to 20,113 and in the previous year, 22,132. A probable reason for the difference, not so far mentioned, is that Steyning, an ancient market town, shares with its neighbouring parish of Bramber some delightful mediaeval features and a magnificent Norman Church. With easy access to the South Downs, it would be surprising if there were not a strong element of visitor attraction, all of which would account for many of the tickets collected having been purchased in the London area and the Home Counties. Sometimes they would have been from locations far removed from West Sussex.

Traffic originating on the Steyning line for main line services was taken into account as *contributory revenue* (see Chapter 7), while that originating on other parts of the rail network for destinations on the branch, or was "throughput", would have contributed revenue not to the Steyning line but to the line where it originated.

Conclusion

In this chapter, station records of the numbers of tickets sold and collected over an eighteen year period have been examined. By comparing the known volume of traffic indicated by actual counts taken during the census weeks of 1962 and 1963 with station statistics taken over five years (which included the years when the counts took place), it has been possible to assess what the probable volume of traffic was over the eighteen year period, from January 1948 to December 1965 shown as *Assumed Weekly Averages.* in Table 5.4.

Even if the assessment of volume has inbuilt but unknown quantitative errors, the trends of traffic decline and increase are unmistakably clear. The indication these trends portray is that traffic on the Steyning line increased by a large amount up to the time when passenger services were withdrawn. Although there had been a decline in traffic in the early '60s, this was no greater than had occurred twelve years earlier and was modest in comparison with the subsequent increase.

Because the line was closed in March, 1966, any inference which may be made, as to whether traffic might not have continued to increase as it did in the 1950s, or whether it would have declined, must depend on an examination of social and economic factors and the geography of transport in the region; and more particularly within and between those communities the Steyning line once served.

On 22nd March 1964, the 10.21 Horsham to Brighton train headed by an Ivatt tank No. 41299 pauses at Christ's Hospital. The single line and platform on the right of the picture was provided for special trains serving Christ's Hospital School. *John Scrace.*

On 30th April 1964 at Henfield, Ivatt No. 41301 hauls the 13.30 Brighton to Horsham train. The booking office and main station buildings are adjacent to the down line platform on the left of the photograph. *John Scrace.*

6 THE TRAFFIC SURVEY OF 1965

Introduction

The previous chapters examined statistics from two British Rail sources, from which the reader may now be aware of traffic volume and its parameters on the former direct rail link between Brighton and Horsham. Nevertheless, the picture thus presented would be incomplete without some means of determining the actual journey structures of some people who used the Steyning line in the pre-closure period. This the present chapter attempts to do, its basis being a card survey initiated by the Adur Valley combined Parish Councils' Action Committee shortly before passenger services were withdrawn.

The reason for the survey and the circumstances in which it took place will be considered first. This will be followed by an outline of the procedure adopted for processing

The 16.30 Brighton to Horsham approaching Itchingfield Junction on 22nd April 1964, hauled by an Ivatt 2-6-2 No. 41327. Note the express corridor stock which had become normal on the Steyning line before steam had been replaced by diesel electric units. *John Scrace.*

derived data, after which the reader will find some typical journeys undertaken daily by commuters briefly described. The last part of the chapter will refer to measures taken by the Minister of Transport, Mrs. Barbara Castle, to vary the conditions of consent to the line's closure after results of the Survey had been supplied to her.

The Card Survey

In the year 1963, for reasons which will be explained in Chapter 6, the Railways Board submitted to Ernest Marples, M.P., Minister of Transport, a proposal to withdraw a large number of passenger services on so called secondary routes and among them was the Steyning line. Since, with the exception of traffic to and from Shoreham Cement works, goods traffic had virtually ceased, if the Minister gave his consent, British Rail had the option of retaining the line in service, or closing it.

Two years went by, during which there was a Public Inquiry and, after Mr. Marples had received the report of the Transport Users' Consultative Committee, there was a General Election and a change of Government. Harold Wilson became Prime Minister and appointed a former miner, Tom Fraser M.P., as Minister of Transport. In the autumn of 1965, Tom Fraser gave his consent to the proposed closure.

To J.H.H.Baxter, an Assistant Secretary in the Ministry of Transport, was given the task of conveying by letter, the Minister's decision to the Railways Board. A similar communication was also sent to the Transport Users' Consultative Committee (TUCC) for the South East and published at the principal stations affected. Within a month or two, Fraser was sacked and Barbara Castle took over the reins as Minister of Transport. But the damage was done. Under the Transport Act (1960), a decision of the Minister of Transport (now Minister of the Department of the Environment) has the statutory force of an Act of

A centenary Horsham to Brighton Special arriving at Steyning. Photo: *E. Wilmshurst.*

Parliament and may not be reversed, for this in effect would be to repeal part of an Act without the authority of Parliament. If the public interest lies in an earlier decision being reversed new legislation would be required if the Minister is to be equipped with the power to do this.

Most people in the communities, which the Steyning line served, regarded the decision to close the Steyning line, and regard it today, as an act of vandalism. The author with two colleagues, who taught at Brighton, Hove and Sussex Grammar School, as well as many other people, commuted daily on five and sometimes six days a week between Bramber and Brighton by train, leaving Bramber at 08.02 to arrive in Brighton at 08.24. The train was well loaded and one realised the difficulties which were likely to arise for many if the line were to be closed.

It was evident that the Minister's decision had been preceded only by a public inquiry and the advice of the Transport Users' Consultative Committee (which was apparently ignored). We do not know if Department of Transport officials and those of British Rail at Marylebone had been informed of the trends of line usage revealed by station records. An action committee was formed and a possible way of presenting the facts to Fraser's successor was for the parish councils along the Adur Valley to initiate a card survey of people who regularly used the train services which British Rail at that time still provided.

A postcard was designed which might throw light on what peoples' travel needs were. Unless British Rail changed their minds and decided that the line was a viable asset, the alternative would be to convince the new Minister there was a sound case for new legislation and have the earlier decision reversed.

Survey Procedure

Fifteen hundred cards were printed and distributed to passengers over a two week period in October 1965, and although official permission for the cards to be available at station booking offices was not granted, at one or two a "blind eye" was turned to this and a few passengers travelling on off-peak trains were able to get them. Parish councillors and some regular commuters undertook the distribution of cards on peak hour trains. Passengers usually made it known to people distributing them if they had previously received a card and, except when a card had been mislaid, it was rare for a second to be taken. Of the 1500 cards printed, a few were not taken up and of those handed out approximately 450 were sent in. This was a return of about 33%. A person needed to be sufficiently motivated enough to complete the card and pay the postage! While this may have been a cause of cards not being returned, it had the advantage of discouraging frivolous returns at a time when the public mood was strong. As the cards began to arrive back, some organisation was needed if the information on them was to be properly processed. Some voluntary help was available and after details of what needed to be done was decided, the team which had been formed was able to proceed. The team consisted of from four to six people working each evening over a period of three weeks in the Garden Room of a house in Holland Road, Steyning.

Assessment of Results

Cards sent in by users of the Steyning line gave journey structures by train out and home and usually indicated the ultimate destination. For the reason previously mentioned, individuals' journey structures mainly involved weekday travel at "peak" times. What now follows is some detail of the journeys of passengers who travelled on early trains each day from Monday to Friday and (quite often) on Saturday. The reader should bear in mind that with a return of about 33% of cards distributed on trains having been returned, the illustrations that follow are not necessarily the whole picture.

The 06.29 'Up' train from Brighton
Destinations of People Returning Cards

Originating Stations	Time	A	B	C	D	E	F	G	H	I	J
Brighton	06.29				1						
Hove	06.32	1									
Shoreham	06.43				1						
Bramber	06.53								1		
Steyning	06.57			1	2	1	1	1	4		
Henfield	07.04		1		6			3	6		
Partridge Green	07.07				7				7	1	
W.Grinstead	07.12				8			1			
Southwater	07.18				5				4		1

	Key to Destinations
A	Henfield
B	Southwater
C	C.Hospital
D	Horsham
E	Dorking
F	Three Bridges
G	Croydon
H	Inner London
I	Billingshurst
J	Bognor Regis

The 07.32 'Down' train from Horsham
Destinations of people who returned cards

Originating Stations	Time	A	B	C	D	E	F	G	H	I	J
Horsham	07.32	1	1+			2*		1			
Christ's Hospital	07.41										
Southwater	07.36					1					
West Grinstead	07.46					1			1		
Partridge Green	07.50	1		1		6					
Henfield	07.54		5	1	1	2	1	4		1	
Steyning	08.01		4	2	2	13		8		4	
Bramber	08.03		3	1		8		7	1	1	2
Shoreham	08.11										
Brighton	08.24										

	Key to Destinations
A	Steyning
B	Shoreham
C	Portslade
D	Hove
E	Brighton
F	Lancing
G	Worthing
H	Goring
I	Durrington
J	Chichester

+ Journey began at Billingshurst, changed at Christ's Hospital.
* One journey began at Ockley & Capel, changed at Horsham.

The 17.28 'Down' train from Horsham
Destinations of people who returned cards

Originating Stations	Time	A	B	C	D	E	F	G	H	I	J	K
Horsham	17.28	3	14	7	8		6	2	4		2	1
Christ's Hosp	17.32				1	1						
Southwater	17.37											
West Grinstead	17.42									1		
Partridge Green	12.46									1		
Henfield	17.50				1					1		
Steyning	17.59										1	
Bramber	18.01								1			
Shoreham	18.09											
Hove	18.17											
Brighton	18.21											

	Key to Destinations
A	Southwater
B	Part. Green
C	Henfield
D	Steyning
E	Bramber
F	Shoreham
G	Southwick
H	Portslade
I	Hove
J	Brighton
K	Worthing

Joining this train at Horsham were:-

A. One from Dorking and one from Three Bridges
B. Two from Central London and three from Dorking.
D. One from Victoria, one from East Croydon, one from Epsom and one from Dorking
G. One from Dorking
K. One from Dorking

The 09.21 Horsham to Brighton at Steyning. The locomotive is an Ivatt Tank, one of those made at Derby or Crewe in former LMS days. The Station House above and part of the back wall exist to this day. *E. Wilmshurst.*

A Selection of Case Studies

The 07.28 train from Brighton:

Mr. Archer worked overnight in Fleet Street. At 18.34 he joined at Bramber the Horsham bound train to arrive in Victoria at 20.15 to get to his work by 21.00 each evening. Returning to his home in Bramber, he caught the 05.20 train at Victoria for Brighton where he connected with the 07.28 train for Bramber, arriving there at 07.48.

Mr. M.M.Northover went to Horsham and Mr. F W Ackroyd, joining the train at Hove, went to West Grinstead where he taught at St Thomas More School.

Mr. Peter Beecham of Portslade, needing to be at work in Leatherhead by 09.00, joined the Brighton to Horsham train at 07.35 and from Horsham went on to Leatherhead via Dorking, arriving there at 08.55.

Mr. A. B. Ahern caught the same train daily from Portslade and went to Dorking, while three others from Portslade - a Mr. Ruder, a Mr. Brown and a Mr. Rixom just went to Horsham.

An unidentified person from Southwick bound for Dorking needed to go by an earlier train to reach Shoreham and there join the Steyning line service which would not have stopped at Southwick. At Horsham, the commuter changed on to the next (Sutton bound) train for Dorking.

Mr. Bennett of Rosemary Avenue, Steyning, also needed to get to Dorking by 09.00. The train left at 07.50 and changing at Horsham, he arrived at Dorking at 09.05. Another person went by the same train on two days each week to Epsom and a number from Steyning just went to Horsham.

Leaving Henfield at 07.57 a Mr. Hedger and Mr. Lyons on 40 - 45 weeks each year needed to reach Crawley. A Mrs. Salt went on to Gatwick by the same train. A number of others commuted to Horsham. A Mr. Wilson commuted to Victoria; an un-named person went to Dorking North and others to Horsham..

From Southwater, some people commuted to Christ's Hospital and Horsham while two had need to be in Dorking and so at Horsham boarded the service going to Sutton. A Mr. Murrell also needed to reach Dorking by 09.00.on 52 weeks each year and caught the same train as the people mentioned above.

Comment

No more than 33% of the people who travelled regularly appear to have returned cards. Ninety three people are recorded on cards as having travelled on this train, of whom twenty-seven went further than Horsham, a number of these to stations in central London or the greater London area.

For the earlier train which left Brighton at 06.29, fifty-nine cards were returned and of these seventeen were of commuters bound for London Victoria, (one of these going on to Paddington), two for London Bridge, three for Waterloo, four for East Croydon, one for Purley, two for Dorking and one for Bognor Regis where a Miss Stebbing required to be by 08.55 on 49 weeks each year. She started her daily journey at Southwater and changed trains at Christ's Hospital.

Government Response

Towards the end of the second week of the Survey, when approximately 400 cards had been returned and the Information on them processed, it seemed prudent to inform the late Henry Kerby, Member of Parliament for Arundel and Shoreham, what was being done. This was in the form of a memorandum dated 25th October 1965, which set all the information that had by that date been derived from processed card data. Kerby passed this information to Mrs. Barbara Castle who had succeeded Tom Fraser as Minister of Transport. She responded by asking Kerby if he would let her have the final results of the survey as soon as they became available. When this was done, Mrs. Castle wrote to Kerby (16 March 1966) stating that she had studied the evidence as a matter of urgency and that she had decided that certain improvements ought to be made in the alternative services between Shoreham and points on the line for regular travellers at the morning and evening peaks. She had therefore varied the conditions of consent to the closure to require extra bus services. While this "variation" might have alleviated some of the worst effects of the closure for people travelling to Shoreham, those who had destinations in the London area, and in Brighton, could not realistically use buses. The "replacement" bus services were based on the assumption that, for long distance commuting, buses were an acceptable alternative mode of transport in place of trains. The buses were not, in fact, patronised after the closure.

In a subsequent interview with Mr. M D Wilson, Chief Traffic Officer of Southdown Motor Services Ltd, Brighton, the author was given to understand that he did not know what had happened to all the people who used to travel by train. "Scarcely any of them, if any at all", he declared, "took to using buses".

Conclusion

In this chapter consideration has been given to what emerged from a limited survey of line users which was carried out shortly before passenger services on the Steyning line were withdrawn. A principal result of the survey was to bring to light the journey structure of roughly one third of the regular passengers known to have used the Steyning line at peak times in the pre-closure period. Most of these were people travelling on weekdays and examples of three trains, two southbound, the other northbound, have been given. Only slight information was made available for "off-peak" and the bulk of weekend traffic. Nevertheless, sufficient is seen to have been gathered for it to be known what were the transport needs of people who resided in the growing communities the railway once served. It was because of this that Mrs. Castle decided to "vary" the conditions of consent to the closure, though disappointingly, she did not bring in the legislation that had been hoped for, which would have enabled her to reverse the decision her predecessor had made. The closure decision itself has been seen to have formed the principal background to the survey and triggered a fair response. Without this, in the absence of an expensive and highly organised study, it would have been difficult to obtain in sufficient quantity the information the card survey had supplied.

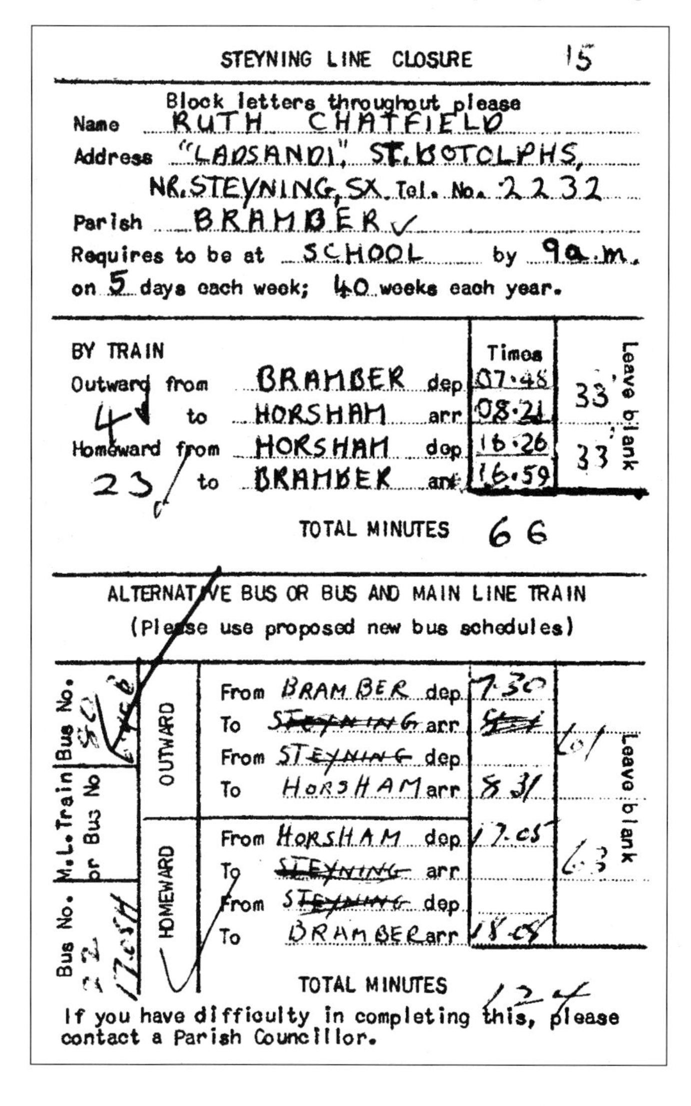

STEYNING LINE CLOSURE 15

Block letters throughout please

Name RUTH CHATFIELD

Address "LADSANDI", ST. BOTOLPHS,

NR. STEYNING, SX. Tel. No. 2232

Parish BRAMBER ✓

Requires to be at SCHOOL by 9a.m.

on 5 days each week; 40 weeks each year.

BY TRAIN

			Times	Leave blank
Outward 4	from	BRAMBER dep	07·48	33
	to	HORSHAM arr	08·21	
Homeward 23	from	HORSHAM dep	16·26	33
	to	BRAMBER arr	16·59	

TOTAL MINUTES 66

ALTERNATIVE BUS OR BUS AND MAIN LINE TRAIN

(Please use proposed new bus schedules)

Bus No. / M.L. Train or Bus No				Leave blank
OUTWARD	From BRAMBER dep	7·30		61
	To ~~STEYNING~~ arr	~~8·~~		
	From ~~STEYNING~~ dep			
	To HORSHAM arr	8·31		
HOMEWARD	From HORSHAM dep	17·05		63
	To ~~STEYNING~~ arr			
	From ~~STEYNING~~ dep			
	To BRAMBER arr	18·08		

TOTAL MINUTES 124

If you have difficulty in completing this, please contact a Parish Councillor.

Fig 6.1 A specimen completed card from the Survey of users of the Steyning Line

It will be noted that the total daily journey time of the person who completed the top portion of the card shown on the left, would be increased from 66 minutes to 124 minutes. The lower portion would have been completed by a member of the Research Team.

7 THE RATIONALE FOR CLOSURE

The Post-war Condition of Britain's Railways
The Beeching Report:.
Avenues of investigation.
Some conclusions concerning "secondary routes".
Some criticisms of the Report
Reasons for Closing the Steyning Line
Users' Evidence for the Public Inquiry.
Further Official Reasoning
Long Term Trends and Line Potential
Burden to the Taxpayer?
Contradictory perceptions.
Conclusion.

The reasons for withdrawing passenger services from the Steyning line will now be examined. One of these was British Rail's predicament in the 1950s of increasing deficits. This was diagnosed and a proposed cure set forth in a report drawn up by Dr. Richard Beeching, Chairman of the Railways Board. This and the particular argument for closing the Steyning line will be commented upon before the chapter is brought to a conclusion.

The Post-war Condition of Britain's Railways.

It was mentioned in Chapter 3 that Great Britain's railway system emerged from the 1939-45 War in a seriously run-down condition.

Nevertheless, until the year 1952, British Rail's revenues were sufficient to meet operating costs without allocating resources for major improvements. At the same time, competition offered by road transport was increasing and in that year British Rail's net profits began to decline. In 1953 revenues were insufficiently large to meet the cost of new rolling stock and motive power units in addition to the cost of track renewals. Nevertheless, ten years after the end of the War, in the year 1955, a programme of 'modernisation' was at last begun. It was applied in the first place to trunk routes with the expectation that increasing returns on the capital invested would follow. This turned out not to be so for by 1960, the annual shortfall in revenue required an Exchequer subsidy of £67.7 million and in 1961 £86.9 million, while a powerful lobby in favour of more money being spent on roads was in the ascendant. It was thus evident that the effects of modernisation were insufficiently rapid, nor did forward projections indicate they were going to be as large as had at first been expected. The Department of Transport and the Board of British Rail concluded that operating losses were likely to go on increasing unless radical changes were made.

The Beeching Report

In 1961, Dr Beeching was appointed as Chairman of British Rail. His brief was

"to initiate throughout the system an examination of the reasons for the Railways' recurrent deficit and outline proposals which, if implemented, might end it".

The terms of reference stated more fully by British Railways were:

"...to determine the extent to which the pattern of railway services (at that time) was consistent with the characteristics which distinguish railways as a mode of transport,

An excursion to Brighton from Oxford is returning on the up line at the Bramber Castle Lane crossing, hauled by a Q class 0-6-0 locomotive No. 36537. *E. Wilmshurst.*

namely the high cost of their specialised and exclusive route system, and their low cost per unit moved if traffic is carried in dense flows of well-loaded through trains."

The Report also said:

"The thought underlying the whole Report is that the railways should be used to meet that part of the total requirement of the country for which they offer the best available means, and that they should cease to do the things for which they are ill suited."...

Elsewhere the Report (p.5) explained that in order to carry out a thorough investigation into the state of the railways, the ideal approach would have been to subdivide railway operations in terms of:

(a) units and sub-units of general managerial responsibility;
(b) function
(c) types of traffic and
(d) parts of the physical system.

A thorough breakdown, which included (a) and (b) could not be attempted for lack of information, although the reasons for this were not explained. Sub-division along the lines of (c) and (d) therefore seemed to offer the most practical avenues for investigation.

Some conclusions concerning "secondary" routes

A principal conclusion in the Report was that if the railways were to begin to approach profitability, certain types of traffic and those parts of the physical system which were "loss makers" would have to be dispensed with. It was considered that if such a policy were adopted, two hundred and sixty-six passenger services, most of which involved stopping trains on secondary routes, would be closed. Those were lines on which stopping passenger services could not be regarded as paying their full cost below a weekly passenger density of about 10,000. Where there was no other traffic, routes carrying up to 17,000 passengers per week were reckoned to barely pay their way.

Some Criticisms of the Beeching Report as applied to the Steyning Line

Because there was a "global" accounting system this may explain why there was no mention of how figures for total revenue and expenditure involving different types of traffic were arrived at, while suggestions about how public transport services might have been integrated were non-existent. In the Report's cartographic illustrations a Passenger Density Map showed the Steyning line *as one of those which carried in 1962-3 fewer than 5,000 passengers weekly.*

Having perused Chapter 4 of this book, the reader will be aware that an analysis of census counts in the same year in which the Report was compiled revealed that approximately 12,615 passengers were carried on the line each week. There were, in addition, freight traffic diversions from the main Brighton line at weekends in addition to excursion traffic from the Midlands, bulk cement movements from the Works at Beeding and of bricks from Southwater.

By adopting criteria based only on one type of traffic and a particular type of function in the physical system, the effect, when considering the usefulness of the Steyning line, was to dismiss factors which would have been seen to be important for the railway network as a whole as well as for the communities the line so ably served.

Reasons for Closing the Steyning Line.

Ostensibly, the basic argument for closure was that the Steyning line cost more to operate than it earned. Information supplied to Fraser as Minister in 1965 included a cost/revenue analysis under Heads of Information for steam and diesel traction, a change to diesel having taken place on 15th June 1964. Table 7.1 shows that Fraser was given to understand that if steam had continued as the motive power the annual savings would have been £173,200 but after diesel trains had been introduced annual savings were reduced to £43,200.

The 09.02 Hove to Three Bridges on 25th July 1959 approaching Horsham, having completed its traverse of the Steyning line. The locomotive is an 0-6-0 C2X class No. 32532. *John Scrace.*

Table 7.1

HORSHAM - SHOREHAM-BY-SEA
"HEADS OF INFORMATION" SUPPLIED BY THE RAILWAYS
BOARD TO THE MINISTER OF TRANSPORT IN 1965

	Steam		Diesel	
Estimated direct expenses	£		£	
Movement	175,000		45,000	
Terminal	34,000		34,000	
Track and signalling	40,400		40,400	
		249,400		119,400
Earnings	53,000		53,000	
Contributory gross revenue	23,200		23,200	
		76,200		76,200
Estimated financial effect (of closure) based on total direct expenses		173,200		43,200

After Fraser had given his consent to the closure, a later cost/revenue analysis was made and is set out in Table 7.2. Inspection of these analyses set out in the manner supplied to the Minister, suggests that according to British Rail's estimates, the annual saving as a result of closure should have been reduced to £27,000.

There is another curious anomaly. Within a year of the second analysis, a third shows a reduced estimate of movement expenses amounting to £37,000 instead of £45,000; terminal

A summer excursion to Brighton is returning to Reading, hauled by an ex LBSCR 2-6-0 'Mogul' south of Bramber. *E. Wilmshurst.*

expenses were reduced to £18,000 instead of £34,000 and track and signalling costs £37,000 instead of £40,400. Had these later estimates been supplied to the Minister before he made his decision whether to give or withhold his consent, it seems that were the line to close, a revised estimate of early 1965 shows that while "Contributory Gross Revenue " remained unchanged,"Earnings" had increased from £40,000 to £53,000 and the estimated savings from closure a mere £14,000. The reduction in the estimate of track and signalling costs appears to have been because the earlier estimates mistakenly included all the costs of maintaining the main line between Itchingfield Junction and Horsham on which Steyning line trains ran.

Table 7.2

"HEADS OF INFORMATION" FOR THE PERIOD BETWEEN CONSENT AND THE ACTUAL CLOSURE

	Diesel	
Estimated direct expenses:	£	£
Movement	37,000	
Terminal	18,000	
Track and signalling	37,000	
		92,000
Earnings	40,000	
Contributory gross revenue	25,000	
		65,000
Estimated financial effect based on total direct expenses		27,000*

* The actual figure stated in the table supplied is £58,000. Beneath an additional "Head", instead of £65,000 a figure of £34,000 is given as "Expected loss in Total Revenue".

SOURCE: Office of the General Manager, British Rail Southern Region

As the reader will have observed, the heads of information supplied to the Minister, and used by British Rail for its own assessment of the case, included an element of track renewal costs. This is a matter which Joy[1] investigated in some depth. He examined the minimum cost of permanent way and found that British Rail's costing appears to be inflated, pointing out that "in the USA, railways under profit-maximising managements are able to maintain permanent way carrying an average density of traffic higher than that of any British Railways' Region at up to 50 per cent less than the cost of the lowest category track on British Railways." This raises serious doubts about the validity of the figures used to justify the policies of the Beeching era. It would then imply that there was still room for a reduction in costs, to an extent that the Steyning line *could have been in profit,* even allowing for the maintenance of the route as a double tracked line, instead of converting it to single tracked working.

What also seems not to have been taken into account was the amount of traffic that was fed into main line working - and cut off when passenger services were withdrawn.

Users' Evidence for the Public Inquiry

A statutory provision enabled people to write to an Area Advisory Committee explaining hardship they would suffer if passenger services were to be withdrawn from a line of railway. In the case of the threatened closure of the Steyning line, two hundred and eighty nine letters

[1]Joy, S. (1964) British Railways' track costs Journal of Industrial Economics. 13, pp 74-89.

An excursion special is passing through Partridge Green hauled by a SRN class 2-6-0 No. 31866. *E. Wilmshurst.*

from statutory objectors were sent to the Committee for the South East Region. After the Committee had examined them, the letters were forwarded to the Railways Board for comment before a Public Inquiry held in Steyning on Wednesday, 26th February 1964, under the Chairmanship of Captain E.H Longsdon R.N.(Ret'd). One of the letters claiming hardship had expressed a problem shared by the author and two colleagues who taught at Brighton, Hove and Sussex Grammar School, now a Sixth Form College, who commuted by train from Bramber to Brighton.

The main point established was that, if it became necessary to rely on buses for daily travel during school terms, the *additional time* that would be spent in travel, in one school year of 40 weeks would amount to the equivalent of *34 eight hour working days.* In advance of the Public Inquiry by the TUCC the comment of British Rail was that *"This position is admitted"*.

Since the sole function of the TUCC was to assess and report to the Minister on the hardship individuals would suffer if the line were to close, British Rail's economic case set out earlier in this chapter was not brought into the public arena.

After the Inquiry the Committee, having considered all the evidence submitted to them, reported to the Minister that they were satisfied that no existing or proposed additional bus services would alleviate hardship for people who at that time were using the train services on the Steyning line to reach their places of employment. The line therefore continued to be used while, at the Minister's request, further studies were made.

Further Official Reasoning - correspondence concerning issues raised

The TUCC having undertaken "further studies" and made their findings known, J.H.H.Baxter, Assistant Secretary in the Ministry of Transport, early in1965 drew the attention of the Board of British Rail to: "...the difficulty of providing adequate alternative services" and that since dieselisation had reduced expected savings from £208,000 to £78,000 (see Table 7.1 referred to above), while this is still a substantial figure, *"in view of the high user of the service, we wonder if the annual deficit could be eliminated by as much as 2s. per journey."*

Baxter then questioned whether *"the argument in this case that custom would be lost would in fact be so in view of the alternatives not being good and for people making long journeys are pretty poor".*

He then put forward the view that since the quarterly bus season ticket was about to rise by ten per cent, the Ministry considered the Steyning to Horsham return bus fare of 5s.3d. made an economic rate for rail of 6s.6d. also a reasonable one. In conclusion, he asked if it would not be possible for fewer trains to run at peak hours and whether the Bramber stop might not be cut out.

To this and to other suggestions about possible economies the reply Baxter received was unaccommodating and facetious, apparently ignoring what had been said or perhaps the official who wrote to him was unaware of the levels to which fares had been raised in 100 years (Plate 1, Chapter 1). He was also evidently unaware of the trend in the public's use of the line shown in Fig 4.1. Answering Baxter's points about possible fare increases nothing was said about possible economies.

He then went on to say that in the Board's opinion

"To make good the loss on the branch under present diesel working, provided there is no loss of traffic, we calculate that ordinary passenger fares, based on 3d. per mile, and reduced fares less than this, would all need to be 6d per mile i.e., double the present standard charge. All cheap fares as such would have to be withdrawn and any cheap fares over the branch would need to be based on the full fare to the branch junction station and any reduction given being in respect of travel off the branch only".

In the summer of 1964, the late Harold Wilson became Prime Minister and Tom Fraser, a former miner, replaced Marples as Minister of Transport. Very soon Fraser was at logger-heads with cabinet colleagues and he did not get on at all well with Wilson. Having a small majority in the House the cabinet, after a number of years in the wilderness and new to Office, would have relied heavily for accurate information and advice on their senior civil servants. Doubtless influenced by his Permanent Secretary, Sir Thomas Padmore, who would have trusted the accuracy of the Heads of Information passed to him by British Rail, Fraser in September 1965 gave his consent to the proposed closure. Baxter duly informed the Railways Board and then had the unenviable task of conveying to the public on 6th September 1965 the Minister's consent to the closure. When notices announcing this appeared in the Press and at stations served by the Steyning line, numbers of people wrote letters protesting at the decision. In reply to G. M. Tovey of Steyning, R. Beal, wrote: "The introduction of faster diesel trains did not attract users back to the line when the numbers fell off... and in view of *the small numbers using the line* the Minister decided that the right course would be to agree to the Railways Board proposal."

Beal's reference to "small numbers", as a view to be taken seriously, is contradicted by "in view of the high user of the service" (Baxter - see above) and appears to have been based on some officials' obsession with the reduced number of season tickets issued, to which reference has been made in Chapter 5. Beal's defence of the closure decision on the grounds that "the introduction of diesel trains did not attract users back to the line" is not supported by the statistics of tickets issued which in the year 1965 had climbed back to a slightly greater number than in 1962; nor by the statistics of tickets collected for which an upward trend was evident and were some 20,000 more in number in 1965 than were sold -

The Battle of Britain class 34050 *'Royal Observer Corps'* hauling the Locomotive Club of Great Britain's 'Wealdsman Rail Tour' on 13th June 1965. The tour covered lines in Sussex scheduled for closure on that date but because of problems with replacement bus services the Steyning line was reprieved until 19th March 1966. *Peter Freund by courtesy of Steyning Museum.*

obviously purchased at stations or travel agents elsewhere than on the Steyning line itself.

Long Term Trends and Line Potential

Either officials of the Board and civil servants did not consider station records to be significant or they may have been unaware of their existence. The significance continually placed by the Railways Board and the Ministry on "declining traffic" suggests that, as has been mentioned earlier, their perception of "falling traffic" was prompted by the decline in the numbers of quarterly season tickets taken up and perhaps on account of the schools' half term break; also by the 1964 November census count which omitted the best part of 1000 journeys undertaken on the line during that census week.

British Rail based its case for closure on a decline in the number of season tickets issued on the line arguing that this indicated a general decline in traffic. At the TUCC's Public Inquiry, Weedon emphasised the position concerning season tickets to the exclusion of all other evidence of traffic. Other British Rail sources, however, do not bear this out. It is true that in 1962 there was a drop in the number of weekly season tickets issued from 907 to 668 but then they increased to 856 in1963 and to 955 in 1964. The picture for quarterly and other season tickets is that there was a modest decline from 1536 issued in 1961 to 1523 in 1962, to 1415 in 1963 and 1394 in 1964. However, the reader will have seen that station records gave a clear indication that, after a short blip, in 1964-5 ordinary tickets issued and returned were again on the increase.

The decline in quarterly season tickets sales will have been because from the mid 1950's, most people in employment had been working a five day week. The illustration below gives three examples of cost differentials for journeys into Brighton using cheap day tickets for five days a week and, alternately, quarterly seasons.

Table 7.3

	Cheap-day return costs		Season Ticket	
	Daily	Weekly	Quarterly	Quarterly
Henfield	3s. 4d	16s. 8d	£10	£12. 17s
Steyning	3s. 3d	16s. 3d	£9. 15s	£10. 19s
Bramber	3s. 2d	15s. 10d	£9. 10s	£10.6s

In the case of Henfield, a simple calculation shows that the saving each quarter, using cheap day tickets for five days a week instead of season tickets would have been £2. 17s It seems likely, therefore, that a person who travelled from Henfield to Brighton and back on five days a week only, would have used cheap day tickets since there was no time restriction on their use.

With the shift of insurance and some other offices out of London to locations such as Horsham and with increasing employment opportunities at work centres such as Gatwick Airport, Crawley, Newhaven and the South Coast conurbation well established by 1966, (South East Joint Planning Team, 1971), the increasing use of day return tickets suggests that some significance should have been placed upon them. For while "day returns" could not be used for travel to London termini during peak hours, there was no restriction on their use during those times to or from other stations in the regional network. Commuters to London, of course, would have continued to use season tickets.

Table 7.4

SOME FARE INCREASES OVER 100 YEARS

A. BRIGHTON - STEYNING

	1861	1963	Amount of Increase	Increase %
Second class return	30d	39d	9d	30
Second class single	20d	33d	13d	68
First class return	39d	59d	20d	51
First class single	26d	50d	24d	92

B. BRIGHTON - HENFIELD

	1861	1963	Amount of Increase	Increase %
Second class return	40d	40d	zero	0
Second class single	27d	45d	18d	66
First class return	54d	60d	6d	11
First class single	36d	68d	32d	90

Sources: Bramber Museum and British Rail

Referring to "possible fare increases" for eliminating the deficit, in their reply to Baxter's communication cited earlier in this chapter, no mention was made by the Railways Board official of any thought having been given to his suggestions, other than to the possibility of increasing fare revenue on the line. In any case the later cost analyses (Tables 2 and 3) indicate that the amount that would have to be raised was overstated.

Be that as it may, on the basis of fares charged in 1861, when the line opened, and the fares charged in 1963, it seems reasonable to suggest that British Rail was not charging realistic amounts in all cases to meet its costs. For example, the second class fare between Steyning and Brighton had undergone a 30% increase in 100 years in comparison with a 92% increase in the first class fare. Astonishingly, between Henfield and Brighton the second class fare had remained unchanged (Table 6.4). In all probability, the officials concerned were unaware of what they might have learned from a visit to Bramber Museum.

"Burden to the Taxpayer" It is not possible to say with certainty whether the exclusion of freight traffic revenue from the "Heads of Information" supplied to the Minister (Table 6.1) distorted the overall view of the economics of the Steyning line. Whether the continued operation of the line, excluding the element of freight revenue, need have been a "*continuing financial burden*" (Swingler) is a matter for conjecture. Weedon, at the TUCC's Public Inquiry referred to the fact that, if necessary, a subsidy to Southdown would be provided by the Railways Board for the alternative services they were to provide but this was not thought to be great. (In fact, Southdown expected their additional costs, £21,000 annually[2], to be amply met from increased fare revenue). In Section 34 of the Transport Act of 1968, meeting these costs by subsidy became the responsibility of the local authority, in this case the West Sussex County Council. M.D.Wilson, Chief Traffic Officer of Southdown Motor Services, in a personal communication, informed the author that where revenue was less than half the cost of operation services were later withdrawn. This applied to Services 80A and 80X which operated between Steyning and Horsham.

[2] See facsimile of a letter in 'Notes' at the end of this chapter.

Contradictory perceptions

In reply to letters received by the Ministry after the closure decision had been announced, that from Swingler is almost in a standard form:

" the Minister only reached his decision after a careful assessment of all relevant issues."

This is in contrast with what Harris, another official in the Ministry, subsequently wrote to Kerby on 31st January, 1966:

" The position is that information is still incomplete as some of the data sheets, I believe, have been borrowed by the West Sussex County Council. It would help if these gaps could be filled quickly. Plainly it is advantageous to have the information before us as complete as possible, in assessing what needs to be done."

In addition, Barbara Castle, who had not long succeeded Fraser as Minister of Transport, wrote to Kerby on 3rd March 1966 that she wanted to tell him:

"...about the large amount of information you sent to me recently on the needs of regular travellers and the journeys they would be making when the closure took place. The amount of information and the details of the people concerned, their time of travel, their destinations etc., is just what I need when I am asked to consider improvements in the alternative services that will take over when a rail service is closed to passengers."

Three days before the closure took effect (the last train was the 21.28 from Brighton to Horsham on Sunday, 6th March 1966), the Minister varied the 'conditions of consent' otherwise than by way of the (County Council's) appeal in the light of specific evidence recently presented to her." (Communication from Padmore, Ministry of Transport)

Conclusion

In this chapter, the reader will have had the opportunity of examining the reasons why the Minister of Transport gave his consent to the proposed closure of the Steyning line. The belief of the senior civil servants who advised him that closure would relieve the Exchequer of a continuing financial burden was the principal factor, plus his expressed belief that people would not experience undue hardship by having to use buses. If this was indeed so, then it might be expected that people who formerly used trains for their daily journeys would use the replacement bus services. This is a matter to be examined in Chapter 8.

Notes

(1). British Railways' (1963) findings need to be studied in the light of post-1950 transport legislation. The 1953 Transport Act *"did away with the 1947 requirement to promote provision of a properly integrated system of transport"*. The 1962 Act, to set up Boards to succeed the Transport Commission (the Railways Board among them), ended the obligation the railways previously had to carry out common carrier functions. The same Act also created the Transport Users' Consultative Committees whose main purpose is to advise the Minister where cases of hardship arise in the event of the withdrawal of a railway passenger service.

(2). Statutory objectors are people who write to the Secretary of a Consultative Committee setting forth the grounds on which they claim they would suffer hardship personally if a railway passenger service were to be withdrawn. When proposals for a closure are published, a time interval is given within which letters of objection may be sent in. People and public bodies (such as local councils) from whom such letters are received are known, for the purposes of the 1962 Transport Act, as "Statutory Objectors".

(3). Facsimile of a letter to the Planning Officer, British Railways Board:

General Manager
Waterloo
29.11.1964

C.A. Haygreen Esq.,
Planning Officer,
British Railways Board.

Dear Sir,

With reference to your letter of 21st November, we can hardly say that there is no question of a subsidy to the Southdown Motor Services.

The facts are that, to provide the alternative road services, the bus Company would be involved in annual expenditure of £21,000. We think this full amount would be more than recouped from the fares collected, but there is no guarantee that this would actually be so.

(Signed Passenger Officer) For D. McKenna *General Manager*

Source: Southern Region Records, Waterloo. Ref: R15 (4)

Looking north, the mound of Bramber Castle can be seen in this photo' of the track being dismantled after the line's closure. *Photo: Jack Burt.*

8 SOME CONSEQUENCES OF CLOSURE

Alternative Bus Services
The Costs of Additional Bus Provision
Journey Structures and Minimum Journey Times
Traffic Dispersion
Lapse Rates of Traffic
Some Individuals' Response to the Line Closure
Changes in Land Use
The Steyning Bypass
The Downs Link bridleway

This chapter attempts to assess some consequences of the closure of the Steyning line.

These consequences relate to the transport geography and communities in the area the line served as well as to individuals. Reference will also be made to some obvious changes in land use.

Christ's Hospital on 15th October 1972.*John Scrace.*

Alternative Bus Services

In advance of the TUCC's Hearing which took place on 26th February 1964, the results of the passenger load census referred to in a previous chapter were considered by the main bus operator, Southdown Motor Services, who then made plans for new replacement bus services. However, the Transport Users' Consultative Committee found, as a result of the Hearing and letters previously sent into them, that Southdown's proposals would not meet cases of real hardship if the line were to be closed. Southdown then submitted new proposals but when the Minister and the Committee considered them, they found further adjustments to be necessary.

After Tom Fraser had assumed office and given his consent to the proposed closure, and then been replaced by Barbara Castle, Swingler, a civil servant in the then Ministry of Transport wrote to Captain Henry Kerby, the M.P. for Arundel and Shoreham, and in his letter describes what then transpired:

"Consideration by both the Committee and the Minister of these later proposals resulted in some further adjustments being found to be necessary and the results are now included in the additional services listed in...the official letter notifying the Minister's decision to the (Railways) Board. These buses must be available immediately upon the closure taking place."

Meanwhile, the card survey referred to in Chapter 6 had yielded data on the strength of which the Minister required the bus services to be additionally strengthened. This was explained in her letter to Kerby to which reference was made in Chapter 6. An altered pattern of bus services then came into existence after the granting of licenses by the Traffic Commissioners.

However, as will be seen in Chapter 9, after three years of operation of the replacement services, it was evident that far from attracting use of them by the public, there had been a decline in passenger numbers. On being supplied with details of passenger loadings, the Minister again varied the "conditions of consent" to the line closure, resulting in a reduction of what had previously been required in 1971. Even these greatly reduced services were finally withdrawn.

Thus, within five years of the closure of the Steyning line, one consequence of the closure was a very considerable reduction in public transport in the area as a whole.

The Costs of Additional Bus Provision

It was stated at the Public Inquiry that alternative arrangements to be provided for school children were expected to cost the local education authority £3,000 each year and since the 1963 estimate for additional buses was £21,000 annually, which British Rail was obliged to underwrite - a provision which was later extended - the saving from closure indicated in Table 7.2 must have been slight. If the position indicated in Table 7.2 was the true one, then it seems probable that with the provision of the extra buses, and for as long as those buses continued to run, closure of the Steyning line involved the taxpayer in an annual loss almost as great, if not greater, than that which to officials of British Rail and the Minister seemed to justify closure.

Southdown, who were the operators of the replacement bus services, subsequently presented a case for their reduction. In their Report to the Minister, operating costs were presented as being 41.93d (17.5p) per mile, while average receipts two years after the closure had taken place were below this figure for the 12 months ending on 31/12/1968. In an analysis for the different services the average receipts were as follows

Service 21 :- 35.27d (14.69p) Services 22 :- 31.84d (13.26p)
Service 80 :- 24.6d (10.25p) Service 80A :- 12.75d (5.31p)
Service 80X : 0.43d (4.34p) Service 117:- 34.39d (14.33p)

Because so few people were using them, the Minister "varied" the conditions of consent for the closure of the Steyning line, allowing the replacement bus services to be withdrawn. A conclusion one may draw from this is that in view of the positive trend in rail tickets sold and returned at the time of closure (Fig 4.1), the net loss to the Railways Board and the Treasury was possibly greater than was expended on the Steyning line before it was closed.

The cutting south of Steyning Station and Kings Barn bridge being widened to take the Steyning bypass. *Photo courtesy Steyning Museum.*

Journey Structures and Minimum Journey Times

The substitution of bus services resulted in changes in the structure of journeys which individuals, relying on public transport, would in future need to undertake. Journey times were inevitably greater; an example being that of a possible journey between Southwater and Brighton for which, using public transport, there were four alternative routes as detailed below:

Route	Journey times
A. Bus to Worthing then train to Brighton	91 minutes
B. Bus to Horsham then train via Three Bridges	88 minutes
C. Buses via Washington and Steyning	104 minutes
D. Bus to Horsham and 117 bus direct	142 minutes

Before the closure, a train leaving Southwater at 39 minutes past each hour would arrive in Brighton at 24 minutes past the following hour, a journey time of 45 minutes, having called at a number of stations on the way. It is with irony that potential users of public transport in the area once served by the Steyning line might have learned of Fraser's comment to Kerby, justifying his decision to give consent to the closure:

"...*my conclusion was that there would be no undue hardship if travellers had to use buses instead of trains. Having decided this, I could not justify denying the Board - and hence the taxpayer - the considerable financial savings that the rail closure would achieve.*"

And to a gentleman who had written to him protesting at his decision, that "*he did not think an extra fifteen minutes on journeys to work would be a great inconvenience*".

Traffic Dispersion

One of the reasons why bus services failed to meet Ministers' expectations was something the reader will understand as "dispersion". If the authorities assumed that the same number of people who used to travel on the Steyning line would continue to travel by bus over the post-closure network, they would have travelled along different bus routes depending on where their journey started and their destination. A result of this was that whereas before the closure of the line one train conveyed most of the passengers at a particular time, after the closure, the people who would previously have gone by train, for example, from Henfield and Steyning to Brighton, would now take different buses along different routes to their destination. Similar dispersion would apply to northbound passengers going towards Horsham. The inevitable consequence of this, which seems not to have been foreseen, must have been comparatively light loadings on individual buses, with adverse effects on the economy of their operation.

Lapse Rates of Traffic

When a transport medium is removed from the physical and human landscape and is replaced by one that is less efficient, the inconvenience and increased time taken on a journey increases the apparent "distance" covered. A result of this is an increased lapse rate or falling off in the number of people travelling by that medium; this was an inevitable result of the line closure.

Some Individuals' Response to Closure

Responses to a follow-up survey which was attempted in 1968 indicated that, for the purpose of journeys to work, most former rail users arranged with friends or colleagues to travel by car on a basis of shared costs. In the course of time, most acquired their own transport and senior people who used to travel daily to London, either moved their place of residence or retired early.

The station house which included the booking hall at Bramber. It was demolished with the rest of the station to make way for the bypass. *Photo: Bob Matthews.*

Changes in Land Use

Some five years after the closure the dereliction of station sites and of the formation on which the track had lain took time to heal. While there may be a greater profusion of plant life on flanking slopes, where controlled burnings no longer take place, the ecological balance has been changed. The primrose, which once abounded, was very soon on the wane and few are now to be seen. At certain locations on the route of the former railway line new uses have been found for the formation. For example, the West Sussex County Times (1969) reported:

"A number of industrial concerns are already using the Partridge Green station, goods yard and line as tenants of British Railways. Last week the County Council asked them if they were interested in buying the sites. In the area concerned there are two retail coal distributing firms, a crane factory, a sausage making plant, and a firm making cast blocks for specially high heat resisting uses. The owner of the firm, Mr Ivor Baxter, said that he had just finished a contract to supply linings for a new gas works at Oulu in Finland. The Shell petrol company would have sited a large oil depot at Partridge Green had it been guaranteed rail access, but (because of the threatened line closure), Shell abandoned the project".

The Steyning Bypass

One positive effect of the closure was that Steyning, Bramber and Upper Beeding benefited from the construction of a bypass. This, many years earlier, had been called for but after the closure the build-up of road traffic on the A283, carrying through the three communities much of the freight traffic from the Port of Shoreham, made the construction of a bypass an urgent necessity. Even so, Government seemed deaf to the entreaties of the community.

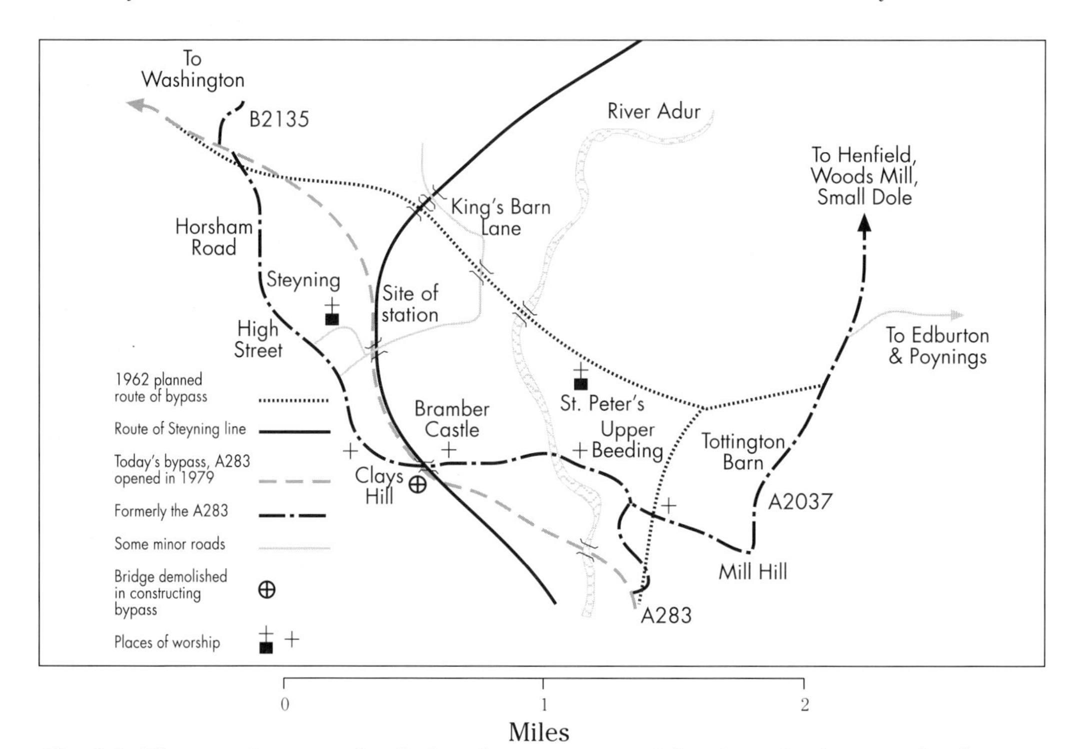

Fig 8.1 The road network of the three communities in relation to the former railway, showing the alternative routes of the bypass.

An up van train approaching Partridge Green from the south. Notice the signal placed on the up side of the curve in the tracks' formation for maximum visibility. *Collectors Cards.*

Two years after the line closure, the 'Shoreham Herald' of Friday, 16th August commented:

"Residents of Steyning have good reason to hope for the completion as soon as humanly possible of the bypass which will divert the steadily mounting flow of traffic from the High Street. The peace of this delightful village...is being shattered by a constant succession of heavy lorries and other vehicles. Much of this is attributed to the vastly increased trade in recent years of Shoreham Harbour and other commercial developments..."

A bypass was constructed and opened on 2nd July 1981 - over fifteen years after the line closure. The original intended route had been to link the A2037 with the A283 NW of Steyning and in 1962 was included in the West Sussex Village plan for the three communities. It would have passed close to the northern limits of Upper Beeding and St Peter's Priory, crossed the R. Adur and the water meadows; then across King's Barn Lane between the farm of that name and the present electricity sub-station, spanning the Steyning line over the cutting just south of Foxall bridge and joined the existing A283 beyond the junction of the B2135 (Fig. 8.1). Included in the scheme was a link road which would have connected the Shoreham Road with the bypass close to the Hyde at Upper Beeding. Government funding for the project had been delayed, it seemed interminably, by which time the Steyning line had been closed. A less expensive option was then proposed by the County (It only cost £3 million!); this was to make use of the cutting and track bed between the two stations at Bramber and Steyning and with Government funding at last being made available this scheme was adopted.

The Downs Link Bridleway

Another positive effect of the closure is that, with certain minor diversions, most of the route of the former Steyning and Cranleigh lines forms the Downs Link footpath and bridleway, linking the North Downs Way at St Martha's Hill, Surrey with the South Downs Way at Botolphs, near Steyning, and on by way of the Coastal Link to Shoreham-by-Sea. This gives pleasure to many people, especially cyclists and walkers.

The autumn of 2001 on the Steyning bypass showing the view north towards Kings Barn Road bridge. Steyning Station once lay just beyond it. *Photo: Author.*

A Lost Opportunity - Integrating Public Transport

A further consequence of closure is that it has severely inhibited any future restructuring of the transport network of the region which, with the Steyning line, would have made possible a highly integrated public transport network. This possibility is explored in Chapters 10 and 11.

Conclusion

In this chapter the reader will have noted why buses provided at the time of closure of the Steyning line were later withdrawn.Greatly increased journey times consequent upon a changed network structure can account for the reduced numbers of people using public transport. The response of individuals to the difficulties of travel consequent upon the closure was, in most cases, an investment in some form of private transport.

The last aspects of the closure to be considered have been to note the land use and ecological changes which have taken place now that the railway has been removed from its formation and the fact that it is now virtually impossible to plan a properly integrated transport system.

The Downs Link cycle path uses this bridge which once carried the Steyning line over the River Adur between Henfield and Steyning at O.S. Grid reference 137 200 (Landranger 198). *Photo: Author.*

9 DIAGNOSING A PROBLEM

Conventional Approaches
Pre-closure Connections between Buses and Trains
Car Parking
The Public's Preferred Means of Travel
Possible Improvements

Conventional Approaches

When Tom Fraser decided to give his consent to British Rail's proposal to withdraw passenger services from the Steyning line, he gave financial losses incurred on the line as his reason for doing so. This view was repeated by one of his civil servants who pointed to the problem of subsidy for the Steyning line as a reason for its closure and that it was unlikely to make a profit *"in view of increasing motor car competition"*.

Motor car competition was undoubtedly on the increase but the view that had been expressed did not take account of the fact that, in the years before the line closed, the author and other car owners known to him used regularly to travel by train between Steyning and Brighton. For those who needed to travel north to Horsham for a rail connection to London during off-peak hours, going by train involved a 20 minute delay at the interchange and 19 and 16 minutes on their return. A commuter taking the 17.29 train from London Victoria would not have too bad a deal. Arriving at Horsham at 18.21 he or she would have only 12 minutes to wait before the Steyning line train left for Brighton at 18.33. However, someone getting the 18.18 train from Victoria would arrive at Horsham at 19.05 and have 25 minutes' wait before departure. So it is understandable that many preferred to use their car to reach Horsham and, having done so, to go much further, to Dorking, Sutton or Croydon. Neither the Minister nor officials in Marylebone and Whitehall appear to have given thought as to how more people could be attracted to using Steyning line trains in numbers they would regard as satisfactory.

It was not only at the Horsham interchange where matters might have been improved. A perusal of rail and bus timetables for the Adur Valley between Bramber and Southwater would reveal how very few were the occasions when trains and buses connected within reasonable limits of time. Unlike on the Continent of Europe, where transport systems are in general well integrated, people who had occasion to transfer from a bus to a train, or vice versa, in most cases would have had a tiresome wait for their connection. And so private transport came increasingly into vogue.

Pre-closure Connections between Buses and Trains

To take interchange connections at Bramber as an example: this was where the No 22 bus service between Brighton, Steyning, Storrington and beyond crossed over the Steyning line very close to the station. Buses from Washington and further west generally arrived in the daytime 15 minutes before the arrival of a train bound for Horsham - but in the evening people would have a 42 minute wait, while passengers from Brighton or Shoreham, alighting from the train and wanting to go to Washington or Storrington would have about two minutes to ascend a flight of stairs and a fifty metre gradient to the bus stop. Before they had reached it, the bus would have left one minute after the train's arrival. At the same time, if residents of

Upper Beeding alighting from the bus wanted to go north to Horsham or London, they would miss the train entirely and have a 59 minute wait for the next one.

So much for the connections at Bramber. What was the position at Steyning, two minutes by train further up the line? Whereas Bramber Station was located where the A283 main road crossed the line by an overbridge, and hence had useful interchange potential, Steyning Station was located at the end of Station Road, a cul-de-sac, and was approximately 750 metres from the nearest stop on the bus route at the centre of town. In the pre-closure period, no buses served Steyning Station directly while bus connections at other stations on the line were no better than they were at Bramber.

The next station north of Steyning was that at Henfield. This was the terminus of the 128 bus service from Brighton through Poynings and Fulking, operated in 1965 at three hourly intervals. On two weekdays and on Saturdays and Sundays, a 127 Service also operated between Henfield and Upper Beeding. The main hourly bus service through Henfield was the 117 between Brighton and Horsham. The stop on this route nearest to Henfield Station was one kilometre distant. Thus, connections between trains and the principal bus service were virtually non existent. Connections between trains and the 128 bus service arriving at 42 minutes past every third hour involved a wait of 42 minutes for an "up" train departure and 28 minutes for a train going towards Steyning and Brighton.

At Partridge Green, passengers from Ashurst, having arrived on a Number 80 bus, had a 45 or 56 minute wait for a train to go to Horsham and thence to London. On their return, they would have a 59 minute wait for a bus to get them home.

Judging from the statistics of ticket sales, West Grinstead Station was the least used on the Steyning line. A reason for this was probably the lack of residential development anywhere in the vicinity of the station. While West Grinstead itself is hardly a village, its station was the nearest one to Cowfold, Nuthurst and Maplehurst. Yet it was there at certain times that good fits between bus and train timings occurred, though not at peak hours. Buses from Nuthurst and Maplehurst stopped close to the station and within four minutes of alighting from it, a person could have boarded a "down" train for Brighton. Similarly, for some "down" trains such passengers as there may have been from Littleworth and West Grinstead Priory had six minutes for their connection. However, this satisfactory state of affairs did not apply the other way round. People alighting from "down" trains would have found their connecting bus had departed a few minutes earlier and there would have been almost an hour to wait for the next. In the case of "up" trains, interconnection with buses involved a considerable waiting time, whichever way it was done. Hence, the efficiency of interconnections at West Grinstead still left much to be desired.

Southwater station was the last to be encountered before the Steyning line joined the Mid-Sussex line at Itchingfield. It closely adjoined the A24 trunk road, access at Southwater being through the booking hall on to the "up" platform. Although one minute separated the arrival times of "down" trains and buses proceeding to Dial Post and beyond, this was a poor connection since passengers had to cross by a footbridge from the "down" platform to the "up" platform, then to the bus stop through the booking hall. For most people, this connection would be missed. In all other cases waiting times varied between 27 and 44 minutes.

Car Parking

While the yard at Steyning Station might have accommodated six cars, there was no official car park and no other station on the line had one. The conclusion the reader will draw is that the railway must have relied for a large part of its traffic on the populace who

Just leaving Southwater on 22nd April 1964 is the 16.21 Horsham - Brighton service hauled by an Ivatt tank No. 41313.The overbridge in the middle distance carried the A24 road and an original LBSCR signal box is in the right foreground. *John Scrace.*

lived within walking distance of a station. Apart from throughput, what may seem surprising under these circumstances, is the considerable volume of traffic that records show was generated on the line.

The Public's Preferred Means of Travel

By comparing the number of people who used to travel by train during week-day peak hours between Steyning and Horsham and those who subsequently travelled at almost identical times by the replacement bus service, it was found that passenger numbers in the latter case were so much less than had been anticipated that they were later withdrawn This can be explained by the time it took for a journey by bus from Steyning to Horsham compared with a journey by train.

The following tables show census figures for the numbers of people who used public transport before and after the line closed.

COMPARATIVE FIGURES OF PEAK HOUR TRAVEL BY ALTERNATIVE MODES

Numbers of People on Board

	Pre-closure train	Post-closure 80A bus		Pre-closure train	Post-closure 80X
Ex Steyning	07.50	07.23	Ex Horsham	17.28	17.25
Steyning & Bramber	30 +	0	Horsham	95	37$
Henfield	59	2	Southwater	84	20
Partridge Green	95	4	West Grinstead	80	19
West Grinstead	104	7	Partridge Green	58	3
Southwater	120	23	Henfield	52	via Ashurst
Horsham	116	21	Steyning	49	2

+ Numbers boarding at Steyning

$ Station or Carfax at Town Centre

BUS AND TRAIN JOURNEY TIMES COMPARED

	Bus Minutes past each hour	Train Minutes past each hour
Steyning dep.	23	53
Henfield	44	59
Partridge Green	56	03
West Grinstead Station	02	08
Southwater	17	15
Horsham Railway Station	33	20
Time taken	One hour and ten minutes	Twenty seven minutes

A useful comparison of use by the public could be made for journeys by bus and train to a common destination if there were some point in the network where journeys by bus and train started at the same place. Such a point was Bramber Station where bus and train departures occurred within a few yards of each other.

COMPARATIVE FIGURES OF PEAK HOUR TRAVEL TO BRIGHTON
BY ALTERNATIVE MODES
Average numbers on board Monday to Friday

	Service 22 bus		Down train	
Ex Steyning	07.37	08.07		08.00
On board on arrival	-	10	Steyning on arrival	49
Steyning Star Inn	10	11	Steyning on departure	80
Bramber Castle Hotel	18	18	Bramber Station	93

Sources: Southdown Traffic Census, January 1964 British Rail Census, November, 1964

For a journey to work in Brighton, to arrive there before 9 o'clock, a person would need to catch the bus leaving Bramber at 07.40.The train which would get commuters to Brighton earlier left Bramber at 08.03. The bus passenger would also have the inconvenience of waiting at the roadside without adequate shelter when it rained. These disincentives or "resistances" to bus travel would scarcely suggest that the latter was an attractive or acceptable alternative for most people. Yet bus services continued to operate and it is perhaps significant that in January 1964, two years before the closure of the Steyning line, only after they had passed Bramber Station did bus census figures for Service 22, leaving Steyning at 07.37 and 08.07 rise very much more than ten.The numbers of people boarding the train at about the same time (Steyning 08.00, Bramber 08.02 amounted to 49, on average, during the census week of November 1964).

Applying the results of computer analysis in another transport field, costing time spent in travel, it was found that train travel between Bramber and Brighton was the cheapest, by car the next cheapest and bus by far the most expensive.This would account for the proportions of numbers of people roughly known to have used the alternative modes of travel before the closure and the use made of bus services afterwards.

Bus and Rail Functional Relationships

It is evident from the earlier part of this chapter that bus and train services were disparate in their function, any seeming fit between them, as at Southwater, being entirely fortuitous. The bus system was a self-contained one, its schedules in some cases allowed satisfactory interchange, for example at Washington between Service 1 (Worthing - Storrington) and Service 2 (Horsham - Worthing). A person from Small Dole, wishing to go to Storrington, could thus easily do so. However, this ideal seems to have been occasionally subject to the whim of bus drivers as reported in a local paper:

On the 2nd April 1966, it was reported that the No 31 bus from Worthing arrived at Shoreham as the No 80 bus to Steyning was leaving which meant a wait of 30 minutes until the 17.36 came. "This is typical", wrote the correspondent, "as buses often depart before the advertised time." Again, on 5th April, "the 17.06 bus, Shoreham to Steyning, departed several minutes early from Shoreham, preceded by the relief bus, which was even earlier. Because of the early departure both buses were nearly empty and as the next bus is at 17.36 quite a number of people had a 30 minute wait at Shoreham."

If we assume that the bus network, established decades earlier, was functionally sound in the 1960s, the imposition of a requirement that buses were to both feed the Steyning line services and be available for off-take as well would have made it impossible for established route schedules to be maintained. It is questionable whether bus services could then have connected with each other where it was necessary that they should.

However, it is unlikely that the bus network was functionally sound even before the closure. Bus census figures for 1964 suggest that whereas traffic volume on Services 2, 22 and 117 made them just viable, Service 80 was already weak and it was this route which was to form the core of replacement services. By 1971, low revenue yield led to drastic pruning of the bus network, already considerably modified in 1969 by reductions in some services. It was apparent that, from a commercial point of view, falling traffic was making most of Southdown's rural network an entirely unsatisfactory undertaking.

The final outcome, therefore, is that not only trains but bus services also were increasingly withdrawn from an important, if rural, growth area of West Sussex. With an ever increasing malaise strongly apparent in the public transport system, the urgent need was and is to find a cure. This requires radical rethinking of what is the proper role of Britain's rail and road networks particularly, in the latter case, how bus services might provide efficient feed-in and off-take for rail services. In the two chapters which follow, the author suggests a way in which this might have been done if passenger services were continuing to operate on the Steyning line.

SR N Class 2-6-0 No. 31866 photographic stop at the north end of Steyning station. LCGB special 'Steyning Line Rail Tour' on the return run from Brighton to Victoria. Possibly the last steam locomotive to run on the line. *J. Bloom.*

10 THE HORSHAM CONNECTION

Changing Trains at Horsham
The possibility of reducing interchange "resistance".
A Model Schedule for Steyning Line Services
Optimum Time Characteristics
Conclusion

The time spent waiting for a train may contribute an unacceptable part of the total time spent on a journey. The "resistance" this imposes to the flow and build-up of traffic needs to be removed if at all possible. When transport authorities examine network utilisation, present policy is to truncate those parts found to be persistently under used. A more rational, and possibly a more effective approach would seem to be to find out where major "resistances" occur, and then to consider how they could be removed. In this chapter, readers are invited to adopt the position of investigators examining the waiting time element and consider how this could be reduced by the rescheduling of train services.

The Rail Interchange at Horsham

The reader will recall that the Steyning line's traffic parameters included an element of non-local traffic which did not originate at any of the stations on the line itself. This traffic, which might be called "throughput", had its origin and destination elsewhere in the regional

Horsham station viewed from the south west. Trains between London, Littlehampton and Portsmouth used the two central tracks while Steyning and Cranleigh line trains usually arrived on and departed from the platform on the extreme right of the picture where sidings and the engine shed were once located. *John Scrace.*

At Horsham on 2nd April 1964. In the siding is the 18.26 train to Brighton headed by an Ivatt Tank wrongly displaying the Horsham-Guildford head code. The 17.34 Victoria - Littlehampton service can be seen ready to depart from the "down" main line platform. *John Scrace.*

network in which the branch functioned as a link. The terminal nodes at Brighton and Horsham, together with Shoreham, were principal points of interchange for passengers proceeding from one of the main lines on to a Steyning line service or vice versa.

Since much of the traffic at peak hours proceeded or originated beyond Horsham, the question arises whether traffic on the branch itself would not have been greater if the waiting times at Horsham had been reduced. Because they were not, the attraction of driving to Horsham or beyond by private car and then proceeding the rest of the way to London or part of the remaining distance by train was considerable. This was undertaken by many; hence Mr. Glassborow's observation when he said *"the motor car was largely responsible for the decline in traffic"*.

Argument rests less on the evidence for a decline in traffic because, as has been seen in an earlier chapter, this was not great, than on the fact that the traffic potential was there and ways needed to be found to tap it. One problem which faces the interested parties, therefore, is whether in any way it might have been possible so to phase the times of main line express services at Horsham and those of the Steyning line, that "resistance" at the Horsham interchange would have been largely eliminated, thus enabling the branch in relation to the main line to be more effective in its input and off-take functions. This in turn would raise the issue of optimum timings for local services in distinction from the global optimum that needs to be considered for the network as a whole.

Possibilities for Reducing Interchange "Resistance"

In order to maintain an hourly schedule on the Steyning line, the turn-round times of trains at Brighton and Horsham varied between four and eight minutes At Horsham, passengers arriving on a Steyning line train were able to join express services to London,

Bognor Regis and Portsmouth as well as trains stopping at intermediate stations between the coast and London. The table below indicates how long a person would have had to wait, having alighted from a Brighton-Horsham train and wishing to proceed to London between the morning peak hour and midday. The second table illustrates the interchange connections in the afternoon and early evening peak.

A	Arr Horsham by						
	Steyning line	07.27	08.21	09.04	10.25	11.25	12.25
	Wait mins	9'	4'	8'	20'	20'	13'
	Dep Horsham	07.36	08.25	09. 12	10.45	11.45	12.38
	Arr Victoria	08.37	09.26	10.18	11.40	12.40	13.45

B	Dep Victoria	15.18	16.18	17.29	18.18	19.18	20.06
	Arr Horsham	16.12	17.12	18.21	19.05	20.12	21.11
	Wait mins	14'	16'	12'	25'	18'	15'
	Dep Stg line	16.26	17.28	18.33	19.30	20.30	21.26

The second table indicates waiting times at Horsham for people having arrived at Horsham and wishing to proceed on the next Steyning line Brighton bound service. Not shown is an exceptionally long waiting period which occurred in the morning peak. If a person arrived at 08.47 from London the next train leaving for the Steyning line left Horsham at 09.30, a wait of 43 minutes in duration.

Could these waiting times have been reduced? An answer to this question must lie in whether it would have been possible to adjust mainline schedules. For a model of greatest efficiency (offering least "resistance") is one in which north and south-bound expresses were coincident in their arrival times at Horsham instead of being separated by twenty seven minutes, as they were. If this could have been achieved, it would be possible to arrange Brighton to Horsham schedules so that trains would arrive at Horsham at least five minutes before a London bound express and leave for Steyning and Brighton five minutes after the arrival of a fast train to Bognor Regis and Portsmouth. Thus there would have been at Horsham a ten minute turn-round time for branch line trains - within the limits of tolerance made possible by the fastest schedules indicated in the Southern Region (1965) timetable, with diesel traction having replaced steam.

The possibility of rescheduling mainline expresses is conditioned by:

1. *Turn-round times at Bognor and London termini being adequate for cleaning and servicing stock and for resting train crews..*
2. *Clear paths being available on main lines.*

The table below shows the 1970-71 schedule of arrivals and departures at London Victoria of principal South Coast expresses. (Source: B.R. (1970) Timetable).

At London Victoria	From and to	Arrive	Depart	Turn Round	
	Eastbourne	27'	48'	21'	
	Brighton	40'	00'	20'	
	Littlehampton	57'	23'	26'	
	Bognor	46'	00'	14'	These trains split
	Portsmouth Hbr	14'	29'	15'	at Barnham.

Any rescheduling of main line trains between Victoria, Bognor and Portsmouth would need to allow for stopping trains' services being so arranged that clear paths are made available. The new fast services could have had coincident timings at Horsham shown in the following table and would need to have adequate turn-round time at terminals.:

Times in minutes past each hour

Times 'Down'	Former	New (+13')	Times 'Up'	Former	New (-20')
London Victoria	Dep 18	31	Portsmouth Harbour	Dep. 23	03
Horsham	12-13	25	Bognor Regis	00	40
Pulborough	27	40	Pulborough	29	09
Bognor Regis	54	08	Horsham	45	25
Portsmouth Harbour	Arr 31	44	London Victoria	Arr. 40	20

Confirmation of "path clear" has involved checking with all other 1965 schedules. For example, a fast train may not arrive at Bognor at 06 minutes past the hour because this would have involved overtaking a coast-line stopping train arriving at Bognor at 07 minutes past the hour. Similar checks have had to be made between Southampton and Portsmouth and between (Waterloo), Havant and Portsmouth.

By establishing a possible arrival time at Horsham, for both "up" and "down" express services on the main line at 25 minutes past each hour, it is now possible to proceed with constructing a model schedule for the Steyning line, the major "resistance" at the Horsham interchange having been removed.

A Model Schedule for Steyning Line Services

The Table below is a model schedule for Steyning line services which could be brought into play if closure had not taken place, or the line had subsequently been restored. It will be seen that trains from Brighton to Horsham would, in this model, be timed to arrive at Horsham five minutes before the north and south-bound express services and depart again for Brighton five minutes after they had left. There would thus be a low "resistance" interchange for both services. The schedule allows for a five minute turn round at Brighton.

Times in minutes past hour

	"Down"	"Up"
Express services arrive at Horsham at	25	25
Revised Steyning line services:	V	/\
Horsham	Dep 30	Arr 20
Christ's Hospital	34	15
Souhwater	39	11
West Grinstead	44	05
Partridge Green	48	00
Henfield	52	57
Steyning	59	51
Bramber	01	47-49 *
Shoreham	09	39
Southwick	12	36
Portslade	15	33
Hove	18	30
Brighton	Arr 22	Dep 27

*Allows passengers arriving by bus from Small Dole and Beeding to board. See Service 'A' in Chapter 9

It will be seen that trains from Brighton to Horsham would, in this model, be scheduled to arrive at Horsham five minutes before the Portsmouth, Bognor and Victoria "up" and "down" express services. There would thus have been a much improved interchange for passengers from the branch wishing to connect with either of the two mainline services. In the model, the departure of the train going to Henfield, Steyning and Brighton is timed to be 5 minutes after the arrival of these trains. Again, the result would have been an interchange facility of negligible "resistance" for passengers leaving either of the two main line services for the branch. The schedule allows for a five minute turn round at Brighton, as was provided for in the 1965-6 British Rail Timetable up to the time of the withdrawal of passenger services from the Steyning line.

41260 Ivatt tank heads the 18.26 out of Horsham for Brighton but wrongly showing the Horsham - Guildford head code on 22nd April 1964. *John Scrace.*

Optimum Time Characteristics

The times shown in the table on the previous page are an approximation of the former branch schedules (B.R.Timetable 1965). An important reason why this should be so is the utility function of the branch at peak hours for journeys to work. An arrival time at Brighton, for example, at 28 minutes past the hour is about right for people employed in Brighton, needing to be at work by nine o'clock. On the other hand, from the nature of most employment opportunities available in Portslade (mainly to be found among items iii to xx of the Standard Industrial Classification Orders, 1966), people would need to be at work by eight o'clock. The arrival of a train at Portslade at 07.15 would probably be too early. However, the train which started at Steyning at 07.34 to arrive in Brighton at 08.00 and calling at Portslade at 07.52 should meet this requirement.

In the case of the global optimum applicable to mainline trains through Horsham to London, there would appear to be an improvement in the timings if the alternative already suggested is adopted. This is because, whereas the former timing got passengers to Victoria at 09.40, the alternative would 'get' them there at 20 minutes past the hour. The global optimum in this case is able to contain a greater latitude of change as it increases the time available for onward travel to employment locations in the West End and Central London. It also improves the departure times of trains for homeward bound passengers from Victoria, since at 31 minutes past the hour, people would have enough time to arrive at Victoria from their offices, assuming that a typical working day for most ends at 4 or 5p.m. A departure time at 18 minutes past the hour would be tight and for those who missed it, there would be a relatively long wait before their journey home began.

Conclusion

In this chapter the reader will have seen the need for reducing waiting times at the Horsham rail interchange, if more people were to have an incentive to travel by train rather than use their cars. The possibility of achieving such a solution, by re-scheduling "up" and "down" mainline expresses to coincide in their arrival times at Horsham, was examined. It was found that this was not only possible but that it could have been done at times which suited optimum requirements on the branch as well as the global optimum needing to be observed in the regional network. This theme continues in the next chapter in which it will be shown how some bus services could have been designed to fulfil a similar function in relation to rail services on the Steyning line.

Note. The term "resistance" used in this chapter is one usually used in electrical parlance. When the flow of electrons in a conductor encounters a resistance, this diminishes their flow and so the current is reduced. This is similar to what happens when people meet with delays in their travel and so select an alternative mode of travel according to its convenience, cost and time saved.

No. 32479 - the 'Steyning Flyer' leaving Brighton at 15.59 for Horsham on a late summer day in 1960. *John Scrace.*

11 AN INTEGRATED NETWORK

New Bus Schedules for Old
Petersfield to Hurstpierpoint
Haywards Heath, Henfield and Brighton
Horsham, Partridge Green and Ashurst
Worthing and Horsham
Horsham, Southwater, Horsham
Conclusion

The exploration of Chapter 10 into what might have been possible in modifying schedules on the Steyning and Mid-Sussex lines can be taken further. Instead of attempting to operate a declining system of bus services which for their continued functioning have to be subsidised by local authorities, if it is supposed that the Steyning line were continuing to function, what is about to be proposed is a group of bus substitution models linked to it.

In these, nine of the pre-closure bus routes operated by Southdown are replaced by five routes, of which some include parts of the old. These replacement bus routes are designated by the letters A, B, C, D, and E, each serving one or more stations on the Steyning line to provide efficient passenger interchange.

Through-ticketing would have needed to be available to avoid unnecessary delays and missed connections. "Park and Ride" facilities would be considered where stations had inadequate parking space for cars.

For the purposes of the model, train timings correspond with those set out at the end of Chapter 10. Each new model bus schedule aims to provide an efficient interchange at each point of connection with the railway network and other bus services. The former Southdown bus routes which ostensibly are to be replaced will be referred to by their pre-closure numbering.

Service 'A' Petersfield to Hurstpierpoint

For years, up to the time of withdrawal of passenger services from the Steyning line, Southdown operated its No 22 Service hourly from Brighton to Petersfield through Bramber and Steyning. For the purposes of this model, the portion of the route of Southdown's Service 22 west of Pulborough is retained intact as also is the 59/61 routes which lay between Petworth and Petersfield. East of Pulborough, the "greenfield" route of Service 22 could be dropped in favour of the route of Service 1 to Washington. This portion of the route follows a belt of almost continuous high quality residential development between Pulborough and Storrington. Between that community and Washington, the overlapped routes of Services 1 and 22 are followed by the substitute Service 'A' and east of Washington that of the 22 route alone.

A Mrs Wright who lives in Storrington, wishes to go to the Wednesday Market in Worthing. She gets the service 'A' bus leaving at 09.12, alighting at Washington where it will arrive at 09.24. She finds a Service 'D' bus waiting and bound for Worthing, leaving at 09.25.

A man from Dial Post, wishing to travel to Steyning, will have arrived at Washington on the same bus at 09.23 and will be able to complete his journey by boarding the Service 'A' bus which will arrive at Washington one minute later. At Steyning the route diverges through

The main building, including the booking office, at Steyning station. *Photo: M. Hudson.*

Church Street to Steyning Station where the Station Yard would have provided ample stopping and turn-round space for a bus. If it is a Wednesday, he would have found the weekly Cattle and General Produce Market in full swing. Some fellow passengers leaving the bus at 09.42 will be taking the train north, due nine minutes later at 09.51.

From the Station, Service 'A' buses return to Steyning High Street and there resume the route of Service 22 through Bramber to Upper Beeding. The old 22 route south of Beeding to Shoreham and Brighton is abandoned and a new route followed through Small Dole to Albourne on the former A23 Trunk Road, now the B2118,then to Hurstpierpoint.

At Bramber, a Service 'A' bus having arrived at 09.47 will depart at 09.51, allowing rail passengers from Brighton and the coast also arriving at 09.47 and proceeding to Upper Beeding and beyond, four minutes to board the bus. This continues its journey past Woods Mill and Woodmancote to Albourne and Hurstpierpoint arriving there in time to start the reverse run at 10.22, after a three minute wait. The service in the reverse direction, from Hurstpierpoint to Petersfield is timed to make possible similar road/rail interchanges. The main rest periods would be at Steyning Station on the reverse run.

At Petersfield, with 26 minutes available for turn round, a rest period could be provided or a short local run might be scheduled. The whole route forms a line of lateral communication between communities north of the South Downs scarp between Petersfield on the Portsmouth line, Pulborough on the Mid-Sussex line, Bramber and Steyning on the Steyning line and Hurstpierpoint.

MODEL SCHEDULE FOR NEW BUS SERVICE 'A'
PETERSFIELD TO HURSTPIERPOINT.
(Replacing Southdown's Service 22)

	Minutes past hour	
At Petersfield Station:	V	/\
Trains "down"		(44)
Trains "up"	(00)	
Petersfield	05	39
Midhurst	48	59
Midhurst	51	58
Petworth	12	37
Pulborough Station	35	14
Trains "up" express		(10)
Trains "down" express	(40)	
Pulborough Station	dep 44	04
West Chiltington Village	00	48
Storrington	12	34
Washington	24	24
Bus Service 'D'	(25)	(23)
Washington	24	22
Wiston Cross Roads	29	17
Steyning Clock Tower	40	06
Steyning Station	42	04
Trains "up"		(51}
Trains "down"	(59)	
Steyning Station	42	49
Bramber Station	47	44
Trains "up"	(47-49)	
Trains "down"	(01)	
Bramber Station	51	44
Upper Beeding Rising Sun	54	41
Small Dole	58	37
Woodmancote Blackstone Lane	02	33
Muddleswood Corner	07	28
Albourne	10	25
Hurstpierpoint, Cuckfield Road	13	
Hurstpierpoint, Willow Way	16	
Hurstpierpoint Church, High St	19 >	22

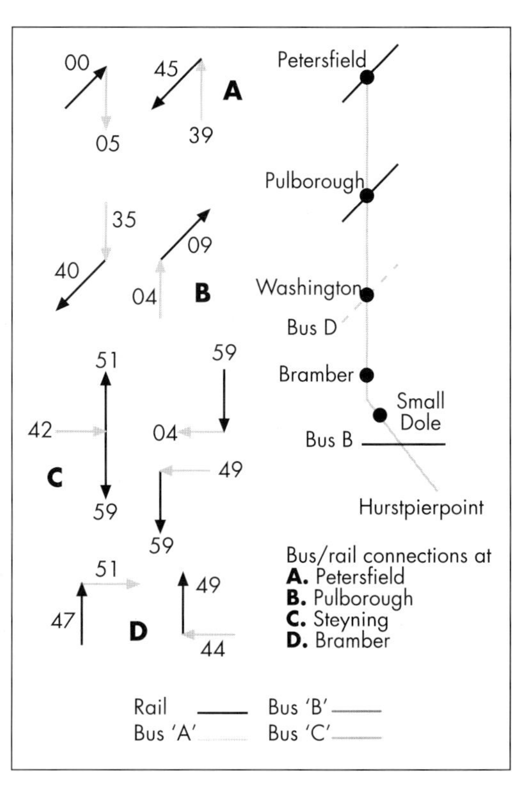

Fig 11.1 Bus and train connections for Bus Service 'A'

SOURCES: Bus time intervals from Southdown (1970) & Brighton & Hove (2000) timetables. Author's calculation between Small Dole and Albourne. Train times at Bramber and Steyning from Chapter 9, at Petersfield from B.R's (1964/5) Timetable; at Pulborough from revised main line schedule in Chapter 10.

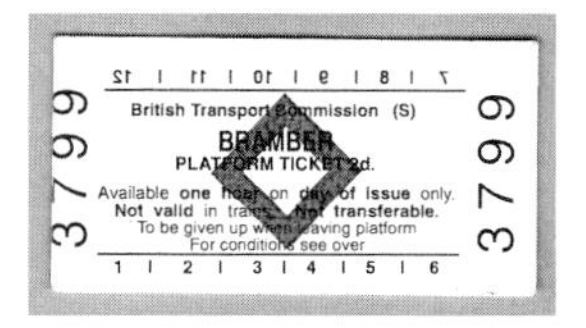

The reader will be able to discern from the table for Service 'A' how the elements in the hypothetical network, if translated into reality, would have been able to provide efficient linkage with rail and certain other bus services.

Service 'B' - Haywards Heath to Henfield and Brighton

The route served by this model consists of the whole of the former Southdown Service 81which connected Cowfold and Haywards Heath. From Cowfold it is extended south along

Bramber station looking north towards Steyning from the "up" platform on 6th March 1966. The road bridge can be seen at the far end of the station beyond the footbridge. *Photo: Author's collection.*

the A281 to Henfield Town - part of the route of Southdown's 117 Service between Horsham and Brighton (now 107 operated by Stagecoach). With Cowfold and Henfield continuing to be thus connected, and with the additional advantage of linking both communities with the London to Brighton main line at Haywards Heath, the route of Service 'B' is extended from Henfield Town to Henfield Station and from there, south east through that part of Henfield known as Nep Town. The route joins the A2037 just south of the junction of that road with the A 281. The route thereafter corresponds with that of Southdown's 128 bus service and the present day 289 service of Sussex Bus from Small Dole to Brighton through Poynings and Patcham.

Model Schedule for New Bus Service 'B"

	\/<	/\
Brighton, Churchill Square	59	51
Brighton, Old Steine	04	46
Patcham	09	33
Poynings Church	27	23
Small Dole	43	07
Woods Mill	45	05
Henfield Station	52	56
Trains "up"	**57**	
Trains "down"		**52**
Henfield Station	03	47
Henfield, Town Centre	06	44
Shermanbury	14	35
Cowfold	22	27
Service 'C' from Partridge Green	**20 - 23**	
Cowfold	22	27
Bolney, opp. Post Office	33	16
Haywards Heath, Bus	50	59
and Rly Stn	\/>	/\

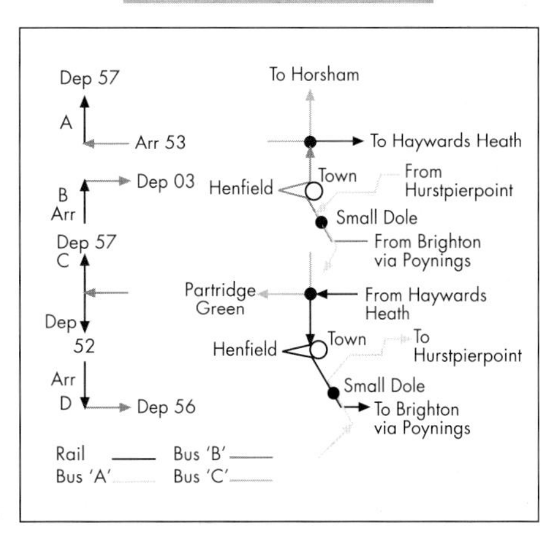

Fig 11.2 Possible bus and train connections at Henfield

Fig 11.2 shows how integration could have worked at Henfield using the model for Service 'B' buses. The time lapse for bus passengers arriving from Cowfold and Shermanbury for the next "down" train would be five minutes and ten minutes for an "up" train, while people from the Patcham/Poynings direction would have five minutes to connect with the next 'up' train.

While a large part of the route of the former 128 Service between Henfield and Brighton is continued in this model, not only would it be possible for there to be an efficient passenger interchange with rail at Henfield Station but also provision is made for interchange at Cowfold with bus service 'C'. The latter interconnects with bus Service 'D' and at Partridge Green with rail. Thus, although changes of vehicle may be necessary at certain points in a journey, the reader will see that it would be possible for there to be a direct communication link between the communities on the route of Service 'B', those served by the other bus routes indicated in the model and the rail network. Normally there would be no prolonged wait at any point where a change of mode might be necessary.

Service 'C' Horsham to Partridge Green and Ashurst

The route of Service 'C' corresponds with the former Southdown's 117 bus route between Horsham and Cowfold, where it is linked with the new Service 'B'. From Cowfold, the route extends west along the A272 until it meets the route of Service 'D' at the crossroads just over 1 km east of West Grinstead Station. At this point it turns south for Littleworth and from there to Partridge Green Station where buses provide input and offtake to rail services..

After a 19 minute rest period, buses would leave for Cowfold and Horsham at five minutes past the hour. It would be possible for Ashurst to be connected to the network by extending the 'C' route to that village and community. In that case, leaving Partridge Green Station at 10.43, arrival at the Fountain Inn, Ashurst would be six minutes later at 10.49. Returning to Partridge Green at 10.50, the bus would draw in at the Station at 10.56 in time for Ashurst clients to join an "up" train leaving on the hour. The bus would then leave for Horsham at 11.05 again with a link facility with Service 'D' from Worthing at the A272 crossroads. Arrival at Horsham would be at 51 minutes past the hour allowing a five minute interval before departing again for its southward run at 56 minutes past the hour.

Model Schedule for New Bus Service 'C'

	\/	< /\
Horsham, Carfax	56	51
Horsham Railway Station	58	48
Horsham, Queen's Head Hotel	02	45
Mannings Heath	12	37
Prongers Corner	08	32
Lower Beeding, Crabtree Inn	21	28
Cowfold	26	23
Service 'B' To Henfield	(29)	
Service 'B' To Haywards Heath		(22)
Cowfold	26	22
A 272 Crossroads [1]	34	14
Service 'D'	(38)	(11)
A 272 Crossroads	34	14
Littleworth	39	0
Partridge Green, The Partridge	41	06
Partridge Green Railway Station	42	05
Trains "down"	(48)	/\
Trains "up"	\/	(00)
Partridge Green Railway Station	43	56
Ashurst, Fountain Inn	49	50

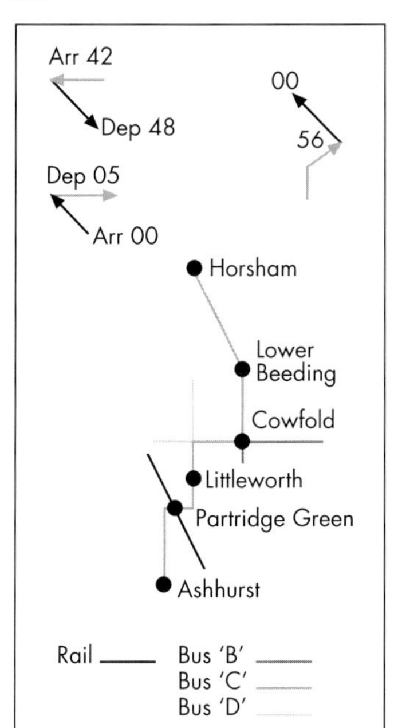

Fig 11.3 Possible bus and train connections at Partridge Green.

Model for New Bus service 'D' Horsham to Worthing

The route of this replacement model corresponds with parts of two former Southdown bus routes: between Horsham and West Grinstead Station through Nuthurst and Maplehurst, the former Service 2, a Southdown trunk route between Horsham and Worthing, the former Service 80 and part of today's Service 108 operated under contract to West Sussex County Council.

The route network is shown in Fig 11.4 from which it will be seen that the model includes a new alignment between Dial Post and West Grinstead Station. There would also be interconnection with Service 'C' at the A272 crossroads to which reference has been made previously.

At Washington, a connection with Service 'A' creates the possibility of feed-in to the Steyning line of potential coast-bound traffic for the Brighton area from Shipley, Dial Post, Ashington and Findon, with reciprocal facilities for off-take, which Service 'A' will have been seen to provide to the west from Steyning and northbound traffic from Findon. Traffic from Washington, Ashington, Dial Post, and Shipley could have been fed into the Steyning line at West Grinstead Station with an adequate interchange facility.

Replacement Bus Service 'D'

	Minutes Past hour \/ <	/\
Horsham Carfax	08	41*
Horsham Railway Station	11	38
Manning's Heath	21	28
Nuthurst	28	21
Maplehurst	33	16
A272 Crossroads	38	11
Bus Service 'C'	(36)	(14)
A 272 Crossroads	38	11
West Grinstead Station	40	09
Trains "down"	(44)	
Trains "up"		(05)
West Grinstead Station	47	59
Buckbarn Crossroads	52	54
Shipley Corner	58	48
Dial Post	06	40
Ashington	16	32
Washington	23	25
Service 'A' eastbound	(24)	
Service 'A' westbound		(24)
Washington	25	22
Worthing Railway Station	52 >	55

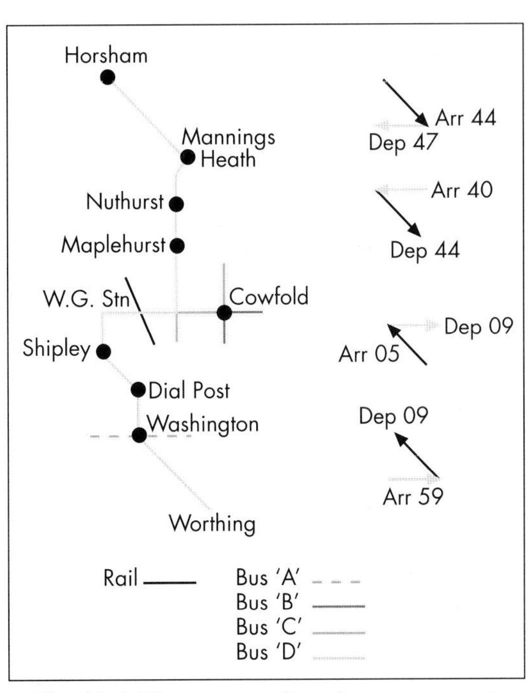

Fig 11.4 Flow nets of train movements and integrated bus services with connections of Bus Service 'D' with rail at West Grinstead Station adjacent to the A272 bridge crossing.

* 27 minutes available for a town service. Service 'D' between Worthing and Dial Post corresponds with that of a fairly lengthy portion of the route of the former Southdown Service 2, until it diverges from the A24 trunk road to serve Shipley.

Two route structures were considered and both would be possible. The first was to extend

Service 'C' from Partridge Green to Horsham via Buckbarn Crossroads and the A24, thus making it a "circular" route with buses operating in both directions. The objection to this would be that such provision would merely duplicate existing and quicker rail provision. A second objection is the "greenfield" characteristic such a bus route would have and very little, if any, additional traffic could be expected to accrue.

Replacement Bus Service 'E'

In the proposed model for Service 'E', part of the route of the former Service 2 is again taken up between Horsham and Southwater. This is a relatively short route which would have two functions: the first being to provide commuter input and off-take facilities at Southwater Station for people who live at a considerable walking distance from the station serving this linear settlement.

The second function of Service 'E' would be for shopping trips to Horsham, Carfax at the centre of the town. Buses would there be able to be available for a town service before the next run to Southwater is due.

The replacement model adopted for Service 'E' would meet the needs of the rapidly expanding community of Southwater. There is no needless duplication of routes, although the probability does arise that some traffic would be generated between Southwater and Horsham, people travelling entirely by bus terminating at the Carfax at Horsham's town centre. There is no reason why this should not happen; for shopping trips into Horsham, bus services would have an obvious advantage and it is entirely reasonable that they should be provided, while long distance commuter traffic may be presumed to be attracted on to the line at Southwater in view of the efficiency of rail connections now established at Horsham Station.

Model Schedule for New Bus Service 'E'

HORSHAM - SOUTHWATER - HORSHAM

	Minutes Past Hour	
Horsham, Carfax dep.	21	51
Southwater Station	34	04
Trains "up"		(11)
Trains "down"	(39)	
Southwater Station	43	13
Southwater, South End	47	17
Southwater Station	51	01
Horsham, Carfax	04	34
Local Service option	V	V
Horsham, Carfax	05	35
Merryfield Drive	10	40
Merryfield Drive	13	43
Horsham, Carfax arr.	18	8
	V	V
Horsham, Carfax dep.	21	51

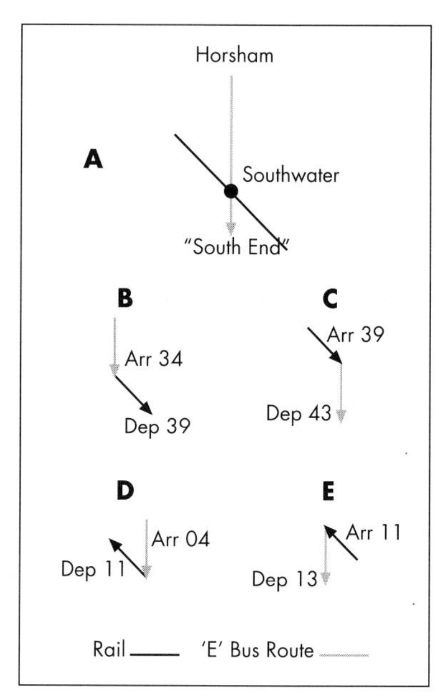

Fig 11.5 Southwater connections cycle repeated

Fig 11.5. shows bus and train connections at Southwater with an extended half hourly Horsham Town Service. (A) shows the route network. (B) A bus from Horsham and

Southwater Street precedes by four minutes the arrival of a "down" train. (C) waits four minutes for passengers alighting from the train and then proceeds to the south end of this linear settlement.

In (D) a bus precedes by six minutes the arrival of an "up" train and in (E) takes passengers leaving the train on to "South End" before returning to Horsham. In order that, at peak hours, "up" and "down" trains might be met for input and off-take at Southwater, a half hourly frequency of buses would appear to be needed. At the time of the Steyning line's closure a large traffic potential occurred in an extensive area of new housing development at the southern end of Southwater. Because new housing development continues at the present time, the need is apparent for an extension of bus services to that area. Details of suggested bus timings are given in the accompanying table.

Note: Bus time intervals are from Southdown's (1970) timetable; train times from the table in Chapter 10, bus schedules by the author, adapting Horsham Town Service No 73 for the local Service inserted in the schedule on the previous page.

Network Integration

An assemblage of all the bus substitution models is shown in Fig 11.6. The significant feature revealed by these models is that bus services could have provided both input and off-take for "up" and "down" train services on the Steyning line. By adopting a route hierarchy in which all bus routes are equally subordinate to rail, points of contact may be found where different bus services can also be integrated with each other. When structuring transport networks, the principle of integrated flow must be observed if, for the travelling public, "resistivity" at points of interchange is to be at an acceptable level.

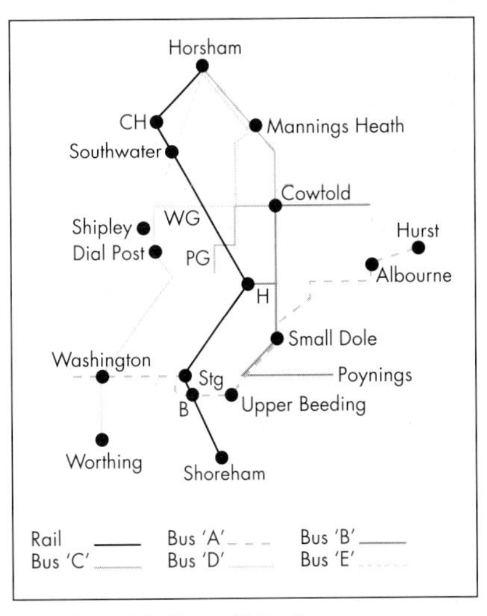

Fig 11.6 Possible bus routes providing input and offtake for the 'new' Steyning line services.

Conclusion

This chapter began with the realisation that both "feed-in" and "off-take" of traffic by buses serving stations on the Steyning line must have been minimal. This was because of inordinate waiting times and as a consequence high "resistance" was built into the network. The characteristics of the whole road/rail network were then examined and the necessity seen for a complete restructuring of road services if public transport was to be operated on a viable basis. After considering what criteria would need to be met, route substitution models were constructed in a way that would satisfy the demands of a viable system. The backbone of a new network was the retention of railway passenger services with new bus routes and services phased to provide both feed-in and off-take for trains. It thus became evident that the possibility existed for an almost completely integrated public transport system between the coastal conurbation at Shoreham by Sea and Horsham.

West Grinstead station from its northern precinct. The A272 road bridge is at the southern end where the booking office was located at road level, making possible easy interchange access between bus and rail services. *Photo: John Scrace.*

An E4 No. 32580 tank heading a Brighton to Horsham train is taking up water at Steyning. The track in the foreground leads to the goods yard. Notice the footbridge in the far distance, leading to the 'down' platform. *Photo: E. Wilmshurst.*

Having just left the Mid Sussex line at Itchingfield Junction the 17.21 Horsham to Brighton train headed by an Ivatt tank No. 41287 is proceeding merrily towards Southwater on 22nd April 1964. *Photo: John Scrace.*

A 0-6-0 C2X class No. 32535 hauls the 09.02 Hove to Three Bridges approaching Christ's Hospital on 29th August 1959. *Photo: John Scrace.*

12 THE CONCLUSION

Summary of findings
Their implications
Conclusion

Closure of this superb stretch of railway came about after the Minister of Transport had consented to British Rail's proposal to end its operations. He had been advised that closure would result in savings of nearly £78,700 over a five year period (equivalent to £2,340,000 at the end of the millennium). In the period between consent being given and the actual closure, it was realised that costing maintenance of track and signals on the line had included the stretch of main line between Horsham and the junction at Itchingfield. The savings estimate, taking this into account and possibly other factors, reduced the figure to £27,000 (equivalent to approximately £1,259,200 in the year 2000). However, the Minister's consent to the closure had the statutory effect of an Act of Parliament. He would have been unable to reverse his decision, even if the new figures had been published. It was then entirely up to British Rail's discretion whether to go ahead with the closure which, having happened, has been seen to be marginal in its intended effect of saving taxpayers' money. Indeed, it appears to have cost the community indirectly more than was saved. For example, an annual subsidy of up to £21,000 was paid by British Rail to Southdown for bus services which were run at a loss.

British Rail's management seems to have had a jaundiced view of traffic parameters on the Steyning line. At the public inquiry held in Steyning in February 1964, the spokesman for British Rail claimed "falling traffic" and, as a consequence falling revenues as justification for the line's closure. The argument was based on a decline in the number of season tickets issued, though the decline had been relatively modest while, as the reader will be aware, the number of tickets issued and handed in in the year before closure was on the increase. The reason for people having tended to buy day return tickets instead of "seasons" needs no further elaboration.

The fact that seems not to have been made known to the Minister and the Advisory Committee was the contrary evidence of *increasing use of the line,* supplied by the monthly returns from each station of the number of tickets sold and handed in at stations over a period of eighteen years, from 1948 to 1965. At the lowest point, in the year 1950, 54,000 tickets were issued. From this number, the total had risen, with small fluctuations, to 116,000 in 1963, the year before the inquiry took place when some 18,000 more tickets were handed in at Steyning line stations than had been purchased. These would have originated from elsewhere on the railway network. After 1963 there was a rising trend in both sets of figures, culminating in 1965, the year before the line was closed, with 20,000 more tickets handed in than were purchased on the branch itself. Combined with the evidence of census counts of passengers boarding and alighting from trains in sample weeks, it emerged that on average more than 12,000 people used the Steyning line each week while Beeching designated the line as one of those that carried only 5,000 and should therefore be closed.

The reader might wonder whether the figures cited in the preceding paragraph were deliberately withheld from Government and public scrutiny? If this was so, what may be inferred is that British Rail's Management under Beeching was strongly biased towards a policy of closing "secondary" routes with no consideration apparently having been given to their future potential. However, station records were able to be examined independently in 1970, when aspects of the Steyning line's history, reasons for the closure and some of its consequences were carefully examined for the first time in the course of research for a higher degree at Bristol University.

An unusual feature for a supposedly rural branch was the peak flow which occurred each week-day, morning and evening in both directions roughly at the same time. Whereas most commuter flows into and out of our larger urban areas, at any one time, is mostly in one direction, this characteristic of Steyning line's traffic suggests that it possessed a higher degree of efficiency, as a network component, than seems to have been ascribed to it. Traffic parameters for individual trains were examined and it was found that most journeys made on the branch consisted of (i) those made from the branch to a primary route sector, or vice versa, (ii) through traffic from one primary route sector to another and (iii) a small amount of purely local traffic on the branch itself. The linking of two primary routes or of feed in to them was thus seen as the Steyning line's chief function.

Tom Fraser's view, that *"no undue hardship would be caused by people having to use buses"* was belied by the fact that most declined to use them. It was clear that even if the level of traffic had remained constant and they had taken to buses, there would have been dispersion of people using them over different routes. Consequently, none of the alternative buses provided at the time of closure proved to be viable. These were all subsequently withdrawn and, in addition, services established years earlier were heavily curtailed. The public's negative response to the provision of bus services was undoubtedly caused by greatly increased journey times. Accessibility between communities by public transport declined heavily and a greater use of car ownership was seen to be an inevitable consequence of this. What has emerged is the fact that neither the former Railways Board, nor officials in the Ministry of Transport, knew anything about the transport needs of people who used the Steyning line up to the time when the Minister gave his consent to its closure, or if they did, the advice of the Transport Users' Consultative Committee was ignored.

Taking the reader back to the pre-closure situation an attempt was made to assess whether, although for reasons already stated, traffic levels were undoubtedly high for a rural branch, it might have been able to attract considerably more if certain conditions had been fulfilled. In the light of this reasoning, the possibility of reducing waiting times at points of interchange in the public transport network was explored. Ways in which this could have been done were seen to be feasible, as an alternative response to the doubtful economic criteria which prompted the Minister's decision. Not only was this so at Horsham's rail interchange, but also at each station on the Steyning line itself, where previously bus and rail connections were mostly non-existent. The condition for increasing efficiency in the latter case was seen to be a restructuring of the bus network.

Five route substitution models were designed to fulfil the necessary conditions, supposing the line to be still operational, resulting in the possibility of an *integrated* bus and rail network in the Steyning line's traffic catchment area. The implication brought out in the study is that where the spine of public transport in a given area is a railway, as was the case in the Adur Valley, bus and rail services are likely to be of greater service to the public and far more viable if they are complementary.

If this had been done when the Steyning line was still functioning, it seems likely there would have been no question about closure; one consequence of which has been to make it virtually impossible, under present conditions, to establish an integrated public transport system in the area the Steyning line once served. And all freight traffic moving out of Shoreham's modernised port now goes by road, no small part of it northward bound on the A283.

Two positive benefits of the Steyning line's closure have been seen to be first, that it made possible the construction of the Steyning bypass at far lower cost (£3 million) than would have been the case with the plan proposed by the County in 1962. The second has been the creation of the Downs Link cycle way and bridle path.

Forty years on from when the author started his 8,000 mile journey to Steyning, the nation finds its railway industry in deep trouble, costing the Exchequer many millions of pounds each year, merely to keep things as they are. Voices have been raised as to whether parts of the rail network should be subject to a Beeching style axe as a way of promoting greater efficiency.

The author believes that while a number of issues need to be addressed, to truncate routes would be a great folly. One of the findings presented in this book may suggest to the reader a need to develop studies of possible network integration. If achieved, this could lead to greater viability of road and rail services, while also meeting the travel needs of people more effectively in all parts of the United Kingdom.

The 09.30 Brighton to Horsham follows the course of the River Adur towards Beeding. The roadworks in the foreground were to do with the new flyover which now carries the A27 trunk road over the Adur. *Photo: M. Hudson.*

BIBLIOGRAPHY AND REFERENCES

Beesley, M.E.	The value of time spent in travelling: some new evidence	Economics 32. 174-185
Barnes, P. (2001)	The Steyning Line Rail Tour.	Philip Barnes.
British Railways Board	Reshaping British Railways (1963)	HMSO London.
Bruton, M.J	Introduction to transport planning.	Hutchinson, London.
Carter, Tony	To the Railway Born.	Silver Link Publishing.
Cockman, G	Steyning and the Steyning Line.	George Cockman.
Dyos, H.J. & Aldcroft, D.H. (1969)	British Transport - an economic survey from 17th - 20th Century.	Leicester University Press.
Henshaw, D.	The Great Railway Conspiracy.	Leading Edge Press & Publishing.
Lisco, T.E.	The value of commuters' travel time. A study in urban transportation. Highway Research Record 245, p.36.	
Marshal & Kidner (rev)	History of the Southern Railway 1.	Ian Allen, London.
Oppitz, L.	The Lost Railways of Sussex.	Countryside Books.
Qarmby, D.A.	Choice of travel mode for journey to work. Journal of Transport Economics & Policy 1.275 -314.	
Reed, M.C. (1969)	Railways in the Victorian Economy: studies in finance & economic growth	David Charles, Newton Abbot.
Sealy, K.R.	Road & Rail Transport in Great Britain. Geography, 69.293-304.	
Simons. J. (1968)	The Railways of Britain: an historical introduction.	2nd edn. Macmillan, London.
Walker, C. (1969)	Thomas Brassey, Railway Builder.	Frederick Muller, Ldn.
White, H.P.	The reshaping of British Railways. Geography, 48.335-337.	

See also 'The Lost Railway'. An 'Off The Rails' (video) Production, (2001)

At the Public Record Office, Kew: BTHR* Reference

Minutes of the Boards of Directors of:
London & Brighton Railway LBR 1/8
London Brighton & South Coast Rly LBS 1/65-71
London & South Western Railway LSW 1/1
Minutes of evidence before a Committee of the House of Commons in the year 1858 PYB 1/89

* BTHR refers to British Transport Historical Records formerly at Paddington.

APPENDIX

A Chronology

1834 London - Brighton line proposed, to be routed through Horsham, Henfield, Steyning and Shoreham by Sea.

1841 The direct London to Brighton line completed and opened on 21 September.

1844 Branch from Horsham through Steyning planned from projected LSWR line to Portsmouth.

1845 London and Brighton Company plan a branch from Shoreham to Steyning.

1846 The L-B scheme receives Royal Assent on 18th June. On 30th June, the London and Croydon Railway is amalgamated with the London and Brighton Railway to form the London, Brighton and South Coast Railway.

1847 LBSCR's Steyning branch scheme shelved.

1856 Steyning Railway Company is formed by local residents but fails to reach financial target. Scheme abandoned at year's end.

1857 Landowners' project, the Shoreham, Horsham and Dorking Railway published on 15th September; Parliamentary approval sought. LBSCR Directors receive news of it and make a counter proposal, seeking powers to construct a line from Shoreham to Billingshurst through Steyning and Henfield.

1858 Landowners' Bill receives Second Reading in Parliament on 10th February. On 12th February LBSCR's Bill has first Reading in the House of Commons. On 5th May the Landowners' Bill is "thrown out" and LBSCR's Bill declared proved.

1859 In the Summer, construction of LBSCR's Steyning line begins.

1861 Steyning line opened to Partridge Green on 1st July. On 16th September the line from Partridge Green to Itchingfield Junction opened.

1866 Two passenger trains collide at Itchingfield Junction.

1867 Drivers' strike.

1880 The line from Shoreham to Itchingfield Junction is doubled.

1914 Ministry of Transport War Executive Committee assumes nation-wide responsibility for all rail operations until after the Armistice of 1918. Repeated in Second World War 1939 -1945.

1942	On 30 November an enemy aircraft attacked Class C loco' No 2308 heading wagons Horsham to Steyning near West Grinstead. Driver fatally wounded.
1964	Accident at Itchingfield Junction.
1958	Regular hourly service established (two hours on Sundays).
1962	November. First census of passenger usage at all stations Brighton to Horsham..
1963	July - August. Second census. Over 12,000 passengers weekly proved.
1963	Beeching Report published, map cites Steyning line as one of those carrying average passenger numbers of 5,000 each week. Railways Board publishes notice of intention to withdraw passenger services from Steyning line.
1964	February. Public Inquiry into closure proposal. In June - change from steam to diesel electric traction. November - third census of passenger usage but Monday to Friday only.
1965	Minister of Transport gives consent to closure. Parish Councils' Action Committee formed, instituted card survey of users.
1966	March 7th. Passenger services finally withdrawn, speedily followed by dismantling of track and infrastructure, leaving single track between Beeding Cement Works and Shoreham Junction.

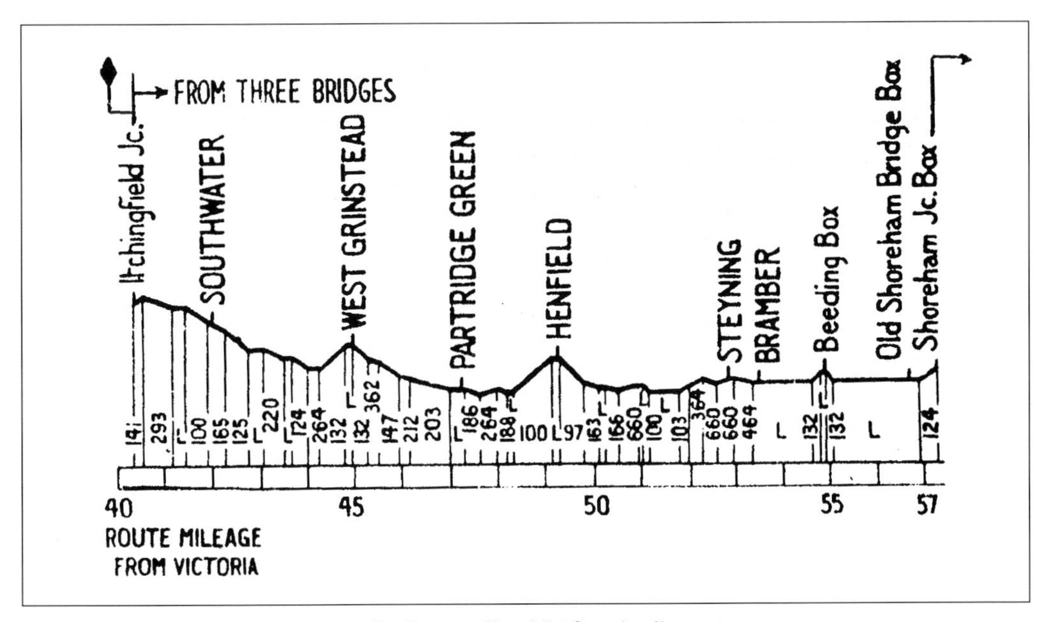

Gradient profile of the Steyning line
Source: 'British Rail - Main Line Gradient Profiles'
Published in UK by Ian Allan Ltd.

ABOUT THE AUTHOR

James grew up on the North Downs in Surrey where a favourite boyhood pastime was exploring country lanes on his bicycle. He has vivid memories of the Battle of Britain fought overhead when he was 16, followed by the "blitz" during which he commuted by train to Forest Hill and later to London Bridge. In spite of war disruption, it seemed rare for a train not to arrive on time.

After war service in the Royal Navy, he went up to Bristol University to study Geography and Geology for a first degree. The year following undergraduate studies was spent in the School of Education qualifying him for a career in teaching. He was later awarded the degree of Master of Science by Bristol for research relating to the Steyning line.

During his time at Bristol he was a member of the Boat Club, rowing in the 1st Eight, reaching the Inter Athletic Union Championship Finals, when unfortunately Durham University beat his crew by a "canvas". Buckman's last major appointment was at Alleyn's School, Dulwich, where he was Head of Geography and in charge of the Cycling Club, leading senior boys on expeditions in, among other places, Norway, Corsica and the Outer Hebrides.

Having now "retired" he and his wife Peggy live happily in Steyning where they are active in the life of the local community.

As a geographer, a Life Fellow of the Royal Geographical Society and a Retired Affiliate of the Institute of Logistics and Transport, one of Buckman's concerns is for efficient transport in meeting the needs of people, industry and commerce. This has led him to write this book which is less concerned with nostalgic memories than with facing the reality of the past as it bears upon the needs of today.